Is Independent Consulting Right For You?

*A Practical Guide for Technical Professionals to Navigate,
Deliver, and Succeed in Independent Consulting*

John A. Paulson

Is Independent Consulting Right for You?

A Practical Guide for Technical Professionals to Navigate, Deliver, and Succeed in Independent Consulting

Copyright © 2026 by John Paulson

All rights reserved.

No portion of this book may be reproduced in any form without written permission from the publisher or author, except as permitted by U.S. copyright law.

Dedication

Dedicated to my three children, Xan, Jazzlynn, and Jaeger.

May you each find your own path, and may the journey be worth it.

Disclaimer

This book is based on professional experience and is intended as educational guidance, not professional advice.

Independent consulting involves business, contractual, regulatory, and tax considerations that vary by jurisdiction and individual circumstance. Readers should consult qualified legal counsel, certified public accountants, insurance professionals, and other licensed advisors before making decisions related to business formation, tax strategy, subcontracting, contracts, insurance, or financial planning.

The examples, frameworks, and perspectives shared in this book reflect personal experience in independent consulting. They are offered as guidance, not guarantees.

Market conditions, tax regulations, and legal requirements change over time. Readers should verify the current applicability of any guidance before acting on it.

Every professional situation is unique. Responsibility for decisions remains with the reader.

Preface

There is no shortage of books about consulting. Some promise freedom. Others promise income. Many promise both if you follow a formula, a checklist, adopt the right mindset, or apply enough confidence and discipline. After a while, they begin to sound the same.

This book exists because independent consulting rarely begins or unfolds the way those books suggest.

For many professionals, the appeal of independence is understandable. It offers the possibility of greater control over how you work and who you work with. It exposes you to a wide range of industries, problems, and organizational environments. Over time, that variety can sharpen judgment in ways a single corporate role rarely can. For some, independence also brings a different sense of professional fulfillment. The work becomes more personal because the outcomes are tied directly to your own decisions, reputation, and relationships. When managed carefully, it can also provide flexibility that traditional employment rarely allows.

Those advantages are real. But they are not automatic.

They emerge gradually, and only after you learn how to operate inside a very different professional structure.

My perspective comes from independent IT consulting, where execution work and advisory work often blur together. One week, you are hands-on inside the system. Next, you are sitting with project managers and stakeholders, translating risk, constraints, and tradeoffs into decisions. Work moves quickly. Expectations are often implicit. Responsibility expands long before anyone formally assigns it to you.

I have been independent for more than twenty-five years. I have worked through strong markets, slow markets, and everything in between, across multiple industries and geographies. Over time, I have seen what works, what fails quietly, and what causes capable people to struggle—not because they lack skill, but because the operating model is different from what they expected.

That operating model is what this book is about.

Although my experience comes from IT ERP consulting, the structure described here extends beyond technology. The same dynamics apply whether you are an independent project manager, a cybersecurity advisor, a systems architect, a developer, a data analyst, a digital transformation consultant, or a supply chain specialist stepping out of employment into contract work. The industries differ. The systems differ. The structural and emotional realities of independence do not. Responsibility expands quietly. Expectations drift. Pricing must align with ownership. Volatility becomes visible. Sustainability requires deliberate design.

I once suggested to a close friend and colleague that he consider going independent. He did not hesitate.

"John, I'm not wired like you," he said. "When the day's done, I close the laptop, open a beer, and relax. You're scanning for your next gig before the screen even cools off."

He wasn't wrong—at least not back then.

Independent consulting is not simply a way to earn income. It is a way of working that demands ownership. You generate your own business. You cultivate and maintain professional relationships that lead to future work. You are accountable for outcomes you do not fully control. You protect scope as conditions drift. You continually reposition your services as engagements conclude and client priorities evolve.

The real challenge is not deciding to go independent.

It is everything that comes after.

This book is written for experienced professionals navigating uncertainty, those considering a move away from corporate life, those exploring phased independence, or those trying to build a practice that lasts. It is not a step-by-step guide. Real consulting does not work that way. Instead, it offers a framework for thinking clearly when the path forward is not obvious.

The focus is on what happens after the decision is made: how independent consultants find work, evaluate opportunities, commit wisely, establish operating rhythm, define their service, manage scope and pricing realities, communicate when expectations shift, and build sustainability over time. These are not theoretical concerns. They are the daily realities of the work.

If you are deciding whether independent consulting fits you at all, begin with Chapter 1.

If you are already fielding calls or evaluating opportunities, the Quick Start addendum is designed for that moment.

Contents

Part I
Considering Independence

Independent consulting begins with a question.

Before thinking about pricing, clients, or structure, it is worth asking whether independence fits how you prefer to work, decide, and carry responsibility. This section focuses on that decision.

Chapter 1
Is Independent Consulting Right for You?

Independent consulting is rarely a first thought!

For some, the question arrives suddenly after a layoff, a restructuring, or a job search that stalls in a colder market. For others, it surfaces quietly as a persistent sense of misalignment. The role still looks good on paper. The pay is fine. The title still carries weight. But something no longer fits the way it once did.

This chapter exists for that moment. Not to persuade you. Not to push you. But to create enough clarity that the question becomes easier to sit with.

The observations in this book come from more than three decades of work with manufacturing systems and over twenty-five years operating as an independent consultant. The lessons that follow reflect situations and patterns observed across many projects and organizations over the course of that experience.

Most books about consulting begin by promising outcomes: freedom, income, flexibility, autonomy. This book begins somewhere else. It begins by asking whether independent consulting fits how you work, how you think, and how you want responsibility to show up in your life now.

Consulting is not a promotion. It is not a lifestyle upgrade. And it is not a reward for being good at your job.

It is a structural shift. An operational shift. A shift in how your career functions, and one your household may need to adapt to as well.

For some, that shift feels like a natural progression. For others, it brings responsibility, uncertainty, and exposure that are difficult to anticipate until you are inside it.

When the Question Starts to Surface

For many experienced professionals, independence does not begin as a formal plan. It begins as a question.

Sometimes the question is triggered by friction. A corporate culture that no longer fits. A manager whose priorities clash with your own. A restructuring that narrows your influence. You are trusted, but constrained. Experienced, but boxed in by process.

Sometimes the question arrives abruptly. A layoff. A stalled search. A role that disappears faster than expected.

Other times, the idea has been quietly present for years. You have watched independent consultants operate. You have wondered what it would feel like to choose your own engagements. You have thought about applying your experience differently, perhaps later in your career, perhaps part-time, perhaps as a gradual shift rather than a dramatic leap.

And sometimes the question emerges not from frustration, but from evolution. Advancement no longer feels like progress. The desire shifts from scale to selectivity; from climbing to applying. You find yourself wanting a meaningful contribution without the full weight of corporate structure.

The trigger varies. What is consistent is a change in alignment.

You may begin to notice that the work you do best—judgment, synthesis, and calm under pressure—does not map cleanly to how success is measured anymore. Or that clarity matters less than speed. Or that you are solving problems competently but not meaningfully.

None of this means consulting is the answer. But it often means something has shifted.

At that point, independence begins to look less like escape and more like exploration.

That distinction matters.

Consulting Is Not an Escape Hatch

Many people first consider independence during a difficult period in their career. A manager who drains energy. A reorganization that makes your role smaller. A stalled promotion. A layoff that arrives without warning. A market that suddenly feels colder than it used to.

Those triggers are real.

The problem is not that they happen. The problem is when the decision becomes purely reactive. Reaction seeks relief. Relief is understandable. But relief is a fragile foundation for a work model that requires steadiness and discipline.

Independent consulting does not remove difficulty. It relocates it.

If you struggled with unclear direction in corporate life, independence will not automatically create clarity. If you avoided difficult conversations inside an organization, independence will require you to have them directly. If you felt undervalued before, independence will expose you to markets that are even more explicit about how they value your work.

Independence magnifies patterns. It does not erase them. A common failure pattern looks like this:

A capable professional leaves a frustrating role and takes the first available engagement because it feels like momentum. They do not slow down long enough to clarify scope, hours, decision ownership, or what success actually means. The first two weeks feel fine. Then expectations drift. Availability expands. The client's urgency becomes the consultant's operating model. By month two, the consultant is working harder than before, with less authority, and with no internal buffer to absorb the pressure.

It is not a character flaw. It is a structural mistake.

Consulting can be a great fit. But it rewards deliberation more than reaction.

Common Misconceptions About Independent Consulting

Independent consulting carries a set of persistent myths. Many of them sound appealing, especially when independence is first being considered.

The reality is usually more nuanced.

Myth: Consulting means freedom.
Independence does provide control over which work you accept. However, once an engagement begins, clients still depend on you. Deadlines exist. Expectations exist. The work often carries more visibility than employment because responsibility is concentrated rather than distributed.

Myth: Consulting pays more for the same work.
Rates can appear high when compared directly to salary. But independent consultants fund everything previously absorbed by employment: benefits, taxes, insurance, downtime between engagements, training, and the infrastructure required to operate professionally.

A sustainable consulting rate reflects that reality.

Myth: Consultants control their schedule.
In practice, the client's priorities often shape the rhythm of the work. Independence gives you control over which engagements you accept, not the daily pace once responsibility is assumed.

Myth: Clients always know what they need.
Many consulting engagements begin precisely because the problem is not

fully understood. Part of the consultant's role is to help clarify the real constraint before meaningful progress can occur.

Myth: Consulting is a lifestyle upgrade.

For some professionals, independence eventually produces a healthier rhythm of work. But that rhythm usually emerges later, after experience, relationships, and boundaries have stabilized the practice. At the beginning, consulting is less about lifestyle and more about responsibility and establishing your practice.

Understanding these realities early does not make consulting less attractive. It makes the decision clearer.

The Hidden Shift: From Role to Responsibility

In traditional employment, responsibility is distributed.

Even senior professionals operate inside a structure that absorbs uncertainty. Priorities may be unclear, but the organization still provides default lanes. The scope is negotiated above you. Risk is spread across teams. When priorities change, accountability diffuses.

In independent consulting, that buffer disappears.

Many people assume consulting means independence from management. In practice, it is independence from having your role defined for you. You may still be hired for execution; however, you are no longer operating inside a role that defines boundaries automatically. You are responsible for clarifying expectations, naming tradeoffs, and deciding what to do when direction is incomplete.

This shift shows up fast for people who have spent years succeeding inside defined roles.

In employment, your value can remain high even if you are not the one setting the structure. You can be excellent within the lane you are given.

In consulting, you are expected to help define the lane.

That adjustment period often feels like this:

You begin an engagement and find that the problem statement is vague. The success criteria are implied, not stated. The stakeholders disagree quietly. The project manager is managing meetings, not decisions. Requests arrive from multiple directions, and none of them has a clear priority. Everyone is busy. Nobody owns the whole picture. You are productive immediately, but you are not sure whether what you are producing is what matters most.

The risk is not that you cannot do the work. The risk is that you do the wrong work well. This is where many consultants either stabilize an engagement or become absorbed by it.

The stabilizing move is not technical. It is structural. You ask the questions others avoid:

- What are we solving first and why?
- Who owns priority decisions?
- What does success look like in thirty days?
- What is out of scope unless we revise the scope?
- How will changes be approved?

Some people find that energizing. Others find it exhausting. Neither response is wrong; it is compatibility information.

Independent consulting is not just execution inside a structure. It is often the responsibility of helping define that structure in the first place.

A Reality Check: What Actually Changes

Independent consulting changes fewer things than people expect, and more than they anticipate. You do not escape deadlines, expectations, or difficult stakeholders. In many cases, those intensify.

What changes is who owns the structure.

You decide how work enters your life. You decide when and how you say yes. You notice when expectations drift and whether you name it early. You protect your capacity, because no one else is assigned to do that for you.

If you have spent a career succeeding inside well-defined roles, this can feel destabilizing at first. There is no manager to escalate to. No policy to hide behind. No organizational momentum to lean on. There is also no one silently redefining your job without your knowledge.

The core trade is simple. You carry more responsibility, and in return, you gain more control.

Who Independent Consulting Tends to Fit

Independent consulting tends to suit people who:

- Can make sound decisions even when all variables are not yet visible.
- Can tolerate periods of uncertainty without panicking.
- Can absorb income irregularity without it degrading decision quality.
- Are willing to name boundaries rather than rely on implicit ones.
- Prefer being responsible over being protected.
- Care more about meaningful impact than internal advancement.
- Are comfortable shifting between roles as situations require.
- Default to action when there is no playbook.
- Balance technical depth with communication that builds trust.
- Are committed to continual learning.

It is often a better fit later in a career, when fundamentals are solid and confidence comes from experience rather than titles.

Independent consulting also does not require a particular personality type.

Some consultants are naturally extroverted. They are energized by interaction, comfortable starting conversations with new stakeholders, and often quick to build rapport across teams.

Others are more introverted. They tend to listen carefully before speaking, process information internally, and prefer depth of understanding over rapid exchange.

Both profiles can succeed in consulting.

What matters is recognizing your natural tendencies and adjusting when the situation requires it.

An introverted consultant may need to be deliberate about visibility. That might mean speaking up earlier in meetings, initiating occasional check-ins with stakeholders, or making sure their work and insights are clearly communicated rather than quietly assumed.

An extroverted consultant may need to slow down at times. That can mean listening longer before offering conclusions, giving space for others to process ideas, or resisting the urge to fill every silence with conversation.

Neither approach is better. Both bring strengths and also have blind spots. The advantage comes from awareness.

The most effective consultants learn how their natural style shows up under pressure and adjust accordingly. They know when to speak and when to listen, when to drive a conversation forward and when to let the room think.

Personality may influence how you approach the work, however, long-term success comes from the ability to adapt your behavior to the situation in front of you. What ultimately matters most is emotional steadiness under uncertainty.

Independent consulting regularly places you in situations where the information is incomplete. A recruiter may say a role is likely but not approved yet. A project ends and the next opportunity has not appeared. A client praises your work but delays a decision.

The consultants who last are those who learn to tolerate that ambiguity without rushing to rewrite the story. They wait for clearer signals before making structural decisions. They keep relationships warm without broadcasting urgency; they resist changing positioning simply to relieve the discomfort of waiting.

In independent consulting, judgment is the real product.

It is rarely a good fit for people who need constant external validation, tight direction, or a clear promotion path. This is not a judgment. It is a compatibility check.

Experience, Timing, and the Path In

For some professionals, independent consulting is not a first step. It is a later one.

Working within a consulting firm can provide valuable exposure before operating independently. It offers a chance to observe how engagements are sold, scoped, staffed, and managed. Understanding the deliverables that are typically required. How risk is absorbed. How expectations are handled when things go off plan. How experienced consultants make judgment calls under pressure.

That environment can be instructive. It allows you to build pattern recognition, client context, and professional confidence while responsibility is still shared. For others, that structure never fits, and independence feels like the only honest option. Both paths are legitimate.

What matters is not where you gain experience. What matters is whether you understand what independence requires before stepping into it alone.

Choosing to build that understanding inside a firm is not hesitation. It is preparation.

I did not step into independence immediately. I first worked inside consulting firms, and the lessons from those years carried forward long after I left.

If you know someone who is already independent and there is an opportunity to work alongside them, take it seriously. As a contributor. An assistant. A subcontractor. In that position, you see how proposals are shaped. How rates are defended. How the scope is protected. How difficult conversations are handled when expectations drift. You witness the parts of the work that clients never see. That proximity can compress years of trial and error into a far shorter learning curve.

Independence does not mean operating alone.

After more than twenty-five years as an independent consultant, I still speak regularly with other independents I have known throughout my career. We compare notes on contracts. We discuss how to structure rates. We share what is working and what is not. We sanity-check difficult project situations and negotiations. We discuss the future of technology. We review each other's articles before publishing. When one of us runs into something unfamiliar, we reach out. When we see an opportunity for a client's need, we reach out.

Just as they call on me, I call on them.

The model is independent. The practice is collaborative.

A Moment of Honest Self-Assessment

Before moving further, pause. Not to score yourself, but to notice your reactions.

As you imagine independent consulting, do you feel:

- Curiosity or urgency?
- Relief or anxiety?
- Interest or resistance?

Pay attention to what feels heavy versus what feels clarifying.

Independent consulting is not a test you pass. It is a model you choose, or do not choose, based on alignment.

Choosing not now is not failure. Choosing not at all is not a lack of ambition. Many highly successful professionals decide that independence does not fit their approach to work or life. That clarity is a success in itself.

For myself, the shift came after a layoff. But it was not impulsive. The idea had been forming quietly for years. The layoff did not create the question. It clarified it.

What This Book Will and Will Not Do

This book will not convince you that consulting is better than employment. It will not promise freedom, income, or flexibility without cost.

What it will do is explain how independent consulting works when it works well, and why it fails when it does not.

If you continue reading, the next chapter makes the operating model beneath independent work visible: how risk shifts, how control changes, where responsibility lands, and why the same work feels different once institutional buffers disappear.

You do not need to decide anything yet.

You only need to decide whether this question deserves a clearer answer.

That clarity is the starting point.

Many professionals assume independent consulting is limited to a small group of senior advisors or high-level architects. In reality, independence spans a wide range of technical and operational roles. Organizations regularly bring in independent specialists to implement systems, solve technical problems, lead initiatives, or provide focused expertise for a defined period.

Understanding this range helps answer an important early question for readers of this book: *does someone with my background actually do this work independently?*

The answer, in many cases, is yes. Independence is not limited to a narrow set of advisory roles. It appears across many technical and operational specialties.

Which Roles Transition Well to Independence

Independent consulting is often associated with senior advisors or architects. In practice, the range of professionals who operate independently is much broader. The common thread is not job title. It is the ability to deliver value clearly enough that organizations are willing to bring you in for a defined need.

Roles that commonly transition into independent consulting include the following.

Implementation and Platform Specialists

Professionals who implement, configure, or extend enterprise platforms frequently operate as independent consultants. Organizations often need experienced specialists during implementations, upgrades, or expansion of existing systems.

Examples include ERP consultants, CRM specialists, system

configuration experts, integration specialists, networking specialists, and project managers. Domain specialists in areas such as manufacturing systems, supply chain platforms, finance systems, and forecasting or planning systems also commonly work independently.

These engagements typically involve implementing systems plus their upgrades, stabilizing operations, or helping organizations extend platforms already in use.

Software Development and Engineering

Many organizations bring in independent developers and engineers to accelerate delivery or solve specialized technical challenges.

Examples include software developers, application engineers, API and integration developers, cloud engineers, and DevOps specialists.

These professionals are often engaged for defined projects, product development cycles, or technical problem solving where specialized expertise is needed for a limited period.

Data and Analytics Specialists

Organizations increasingly rely on independent specialists to help extract value from their data without building permanent internal teams.

Examples include data analysts, data engineers, business intelligence developers, data warehouse architects, and machine learning or AI specialists.

These engagements often focus on building reporting environments, improving data pipelines, or supporting leadership decision-making through better analysis and visibility.

Infrastructure and Networking Specialists

Independent consultants frequently assist organizations with infrastructure modernization, performance improvement, or migration initiatives.

Examples include systems engineers, network architects, cloud infrastructure specialists, virtualization experts, and storage or performance specialists.

These consultants are commonly brought in during upgrades, system migrations, or infrastructure expansion projects.

Security Specialists

Cybersecurity expertise is increasingly engaged on a consulting basis, particularly when organizations require focused expertise for assessments or remediation work.

Examples include cybersecurity analysts, penetration testers, security architects, compliance specialists, and incident response professionals.

These consultants often support security reviews, compliance readiness, vulnerability assessments, and recovery planning.

Systems Architecture and Technical Advisory

Some independent consultants operate primarily in advisory roles, helping organizations design systems or make strategic technology decisions rather than executing the work directly.

Examples include systems architects, enterprise architects, solution architects, and technology strategy advisors.

These roles typically focus on architecture design, governance models, platform selection, and long-term technology planning.

Project and Program Leadership

Another large group of independent consultants specializes in leading complex initiatives rather than performing the technical work themselves.

Examples include technical project managers, ERP implementation managers, program managers, PMO specialists, and transformation program leads.

Organizations often bring these professionals in to coordinate large initiatives, stabilize struggling projects, or provide experienced leadership during major implementations.

The Common Thread

Across all of these roles, successful independent consultants share one characteristic.

Their work produces a clear and identifiable outcome. Organizations can explain why they need them and what problem they are expected to solve. When that clarity exists, independence becomes possible regardless of the specific technology, platform, or job title involved.

Transition to Chapter 2

Once the idea of independence becomes real, the next question is structural. What actually changes when you step into it?

Chapter 2 makes the independent operating model visible: how risk shifts, how control changes, where responsibility lands, and why the same work feels different once institutional buffers disappear.

Part II
Understanding the Independent Operating Model

Once independence becomes a real possibility, the next step is understanding how the model actually works. Consulting does not simply replace employment. It redistributes responsibility, visibility, and risk.

This section makes that operating model visible.

Chapter 2
The Operating Model

Risk, Control, and What Actually Changes

If Chapter 1 helped you assess whether independent consulting might fit you, this chapter explains what independence actually is. Not philosophically—structurally.

Independent consulting is not defined by freedom, flexibility, or even income. It is defined by its operating model, the underlying logic that determines who carries risk, who makes decisions, how value is created, and how failure is absorbed.

Most early struggles in consulting come not from the work itself, but from misunderstanding how responsibility, risk, and control function in the independent model.

This chapter exists to make that model visible.

What an Operating Model Really Is

Most professionals believe they understand how their work operates because the tasks themselves are familiar. Systems behave the same. Tools are recognizable. The people dynamics also look familiar.

What changes in independent consulting is not the work. It is the structure beneath it.

That structure determines where responsibility accumulates, how decisions get made under pressure, and who absorbs the cost when clarity is missing. When the structure shifts, the same work produces very different outcomes. This is why independent consulting can feel disorienting at first, even for experienced professionals.

An operating model is the structure beneath the work. It determines four things.

Where responsibility lands

Who is expected to notice problems, make tradeoffs, and absorb consequences when things do not go as planned.

How decisions get made

Whether choices are made explicitly by identified owners, delayed through consensus, or defaulted to whoever is most available.

Who absorbs volatility

Shifting priorities. Delayed access. Late credentials. Changing stakeholders. Technical constraints that surface mid-engagement. Unclear scope still lands somewhere. The question is where.

How success is evaluated

In employment, success can feel measurable. You may improve uptime, reduce cost, stabilize a system, shorten lead times, or close out a major implementation milestone. You know what moved.

But how that success is valued is often culturally negotiated. It is filtered through manager relationships, internal narratives, shifting priorities, and expectations that change without anyone formally naming the change.

A concrete example most experienced professionals recognize:
> You stabilize a failing system or recover a project that was sliding. The measurable result is real. But by the next quarter, the organization is focused on something else. Credit shifts. Goalposts move. A new leader reframes the story. Your work still mattered. The interpretation changed.

In independent consulting, success is defined first by the contract. Scope is written. Deliverables are written. Timelines are written. Boundaries are visible. There is less room for ambiguity to quietly work in your favor.

But contractual completion is not the full measure. Client confidence determines whether the engagement extends, whether your name is recommended, and whether trust compounds over time. The contract defines the obligation. The client's confidence defines the future.

In practice, that confidence often shows up in simple ways. After an engagement concludes, the consulting firm that placed you may call with feedback from the client. Sometimes the message is brief: they were happy with the work and would bring you back if another need arises. In independent consulting, those quiet signals of trust often define success more than any internal performance review ever did.

You can do the same technical work inside different operating models and experience it completely differently. The tasks look familiar; the structure around them does not.

In independent consulting, the work may look the same, but the measure of success changes. It is not defined by internal narratives or performance cycles. It is defined by whether the client trusts you enough to call again.

Employment, Contracting, and Consulting Are Not the Same Thing

Many people use contracting and consulting interchangeably. In everyday conversations, the distinction is blurred.

But the operating models are not the same.

The difference is not titles or paperwork. It is where responsibility for outcomes resides.

In employment, responsibility is distributed. Even when you are accountable, you operate inside layers of protection: managers, policies, HR, budgets, and shared ownership. Risk is real, but it is absorbed collectively.

In contracting or staff augmentation, the employer changes, but much of the structure remains. You are brought in to execute within an existing framework. Priorities are usually set elsewhere. Success is defined as reliability and integration.

Consulting is different.

In consulting, responsibility shifts upstream. You are expected not just to do the work, but to help determine what work matters, what tradeoffs are acceptable, what risks should be taken or avoided, and how the effort aligns with the organization's strategic priorities.

This is not about intelligence or seniority. It is about where responsibility for outcomes resides.

A common frustration in independence comes from an operating model mismatch. You are hired as a consultant but treated like a contractor: given tasks, not invited into judgment, yet still blamed when outcomes disappoint. Or you are hired as a contractor but expected to operate like a consultant: asked to own outcomes without the authority, scope, or rate to match.

That mismatch is not just annoying. It is one of the fastest paths to burnout and scope conflict. Later chapters will show how to name it early and price it honestly.

One Problem, Three Models

Consider a common IT situation: a system slows down or becomes unstable after a significant change.

In an employment model, you are assigned to investigate. Leadership sets urgency and scope. Communication flows through management. If the root cause is misjudged, responsibility is shared.

In a contracting model, you are brought in to fix what the client believes is the issue. The problem is framed for you. Success means restoring stability efficiently.

In a consulting model, the client may not know the actual problem. Your value lies in determining whether the issue is technical, architectural, procedural, or expectation-based, and then guiding the decision about what to do next.

In the consulting model, you may also have to say something the client does not want to hear.

The thing you called me about is not the real problem. The real problem is upstream: governance, ownership, data quality, process discipline, or incentives.

That is where advisory responsibility becomes real.

The technical work may overlap. The responsibility does not.

Independence of Judgment

Independent consulting creates space for judgment that is not conditioned by partnership incentives.

Many consulting firms operate within formal partnerships or informal relationships with software vendors, platform providers, or implementation ecosystems. These relationships are not inherently wrong, but they do shape recommendations. Certain modules, architectures, upgrades, or tools can be favored because they align with certifications, revenue models, or partnership expectations.

Independent consultants are not positioned inside those structures.

They are not rewarded for selling licenses, expanding vendor footprints, or steering decisions toward preferred platforms. Their value lies in judgment, helping a client assess what actually makes sense given the environment, constraints, and long-term implications.

For clients, this can be the difference between:

- Validating whether an upgrade is necessary at all.
- Distinguishing between a technical limitation and a process problem.
- Understanding whether change is being driven by business need or vendor momentum.
- Evaluating the operational and financial implications of moving their ERP system to a cloud platform.

This does not mean independent consultants are anti-vendor or anti-technology. It means their recommendations are not tied to maintaining external relationships and their incentives.

That independence is often why they are brought in, particularly when:

- Leadership wants a second opinion.
- Previous initiatives underperformed.
- Large investments are being considered.
- Internal teams feel pressure to modernize without clarity on why.

- Internal teams have already committed to a direction and need a politically neutral voice to validate or challenge it.

In those moments, an independent perspective is not about disruption. It is about restoring clarity.

Where Friction Begins

Execution and Advisory Work Overlap

In IT consulting, the boundary between execution and advisory work is rarely clean.

A client may bring you in to stabilize a system and later ask you to recommend a redesign. They may trust your judgment because they have seen you execute. Over time, doing the work quietly becomes deciding what the work should be.

This overlap is normal.

It is also where many engagements become unsustainable if the shift is not named. You may hear phrases like:

- Since you know the system best, what do you think we should do?
- Can you lead this decision?
- We need you to own the outcome

None of these are unreasonable. But they represent a change in responsibility.

Execution, or specialist work, assumes direction. Advisory work assumes judgment and accountability.

You can switch between these modes within a single engagement. But both parties must recognize when the shift occurs. When they do not, expectations expand silently and risk accumulates unevenly.

Later chapters will name these patterns explicitly and show how the specialist versus advisory distinction affects service definition, pricing, and sustainability. For now, it is enough to recognize that the model can change mid engagement, and unacknowledged change is the source of most consulting friction.

The Real Risk Shift

Visible Risk vs Hidden Risk

Many professionals believe employment is stable and consulting is risky. This belief persists even after layoffs, reorganizations, outsourcing, acquisitions, and market cycles repeatedly prove otherwise.

The difference is not the existence of risk. It is where risk resides, and when you see it. Employment tends to hide risk.

Strategy shifts happen above you. Consolidations arrive late. Roles disappear quickly. A reorganization can render your domain irrelevant overnight. A new leader can pivot priorities and quietly devalue the work on which you built your reputation. The risk was there. You just did not see it until it arrived.

Independent consulting makes risk visible.

Pipeline gaps show up in real time. Client concentration becomes measurable. Demand shifts appear earlier. You feel volatility sooner, but you also see it sooner.

Visible risk feels uncomfortable. But it can be managed. Hidden risk simply happens to you.

A simple contrast makes this tangible.

In employment, a slow quarter can exist for months before you know it matters. In consulting, you can see the signals in your inbox, your calendar, and your pipeline and you can respond while there is still time to respond.

Over time, many experienced consultants come to prefer visible risk, not because it is smaller, but because it is knowable.

Control Is Not the Absence of Risk

Independence does not remove risk. It relocates it.

As an independent consultant, you assume responsibility for:

Where work comes from

You maintain visibility, relationships, and positioning so opportunities continue beyond any single engagement. This is demanding early on, but it produces something employment rarely does: a network and reputation that belong entirely to you.

Employed professionals often find their market relationships are institutional, mediated by their employer, constrained by their role. Independent consultants who invest consistently in visibility, relationships, and publishing build a professional asset that compounds over time and travels with them regardless of where any single engagement leads.

How much dependency you carry

You decide how reliant your income, schedule, or identity becomes on a single client, role, or situation, and you absorb the risk of that concentration.

How quickly you notice misalignment

You recognize when expectations, scope, or incentives drift before the cost of staying rises quietly.

When you adjust or exit

You choose when to renegotiate, reposition, or walk away, rather than waiting for permission or institutional intervention.

This concentration of responsibility can feel heavy early on. It also introduces something employment rarely offers: choice.

You can diversify clients. You can change your service mix. You can say no earlier. You can leave situations that no longer make sense.

Risk remains. But it becomes something you work with, not something that surprises you.

A brief note that matters for many households:

This visibility is not experienced only by you. Partners and families feel it too. Irregular income, shifting schedules, and the emotional load of watching someone absorb visible risk can create friction at home even when the consulting work is going well. The operating model is professional, but the effects are personal. It is worth naming early.

Optionality - The Long Game

The real asset independent consulting builds is not income. It is optionality.

Optionality is the ability to make meaningful choices when conditions shift. It is the ability to adjust how you work without starting over, or to step back temporarily without exiting entirely.

Optionality is what a strong independent practice buys you over time.

At year five, optionality might mean you no longer need to accept misaligned work just to keep cash moving. You can wait for better fit because you have repeat clients, referrals, and a clearer positioning.

At year ten, it might mean you can shift from hands-on delivery to higher leverage advisory work without rebuilding credibility from scratch. You can choose fewer engagements with higher trust because your reputation carries weight.

At year fifteen, it can mean your calendar becomes intentional. You can structure seasons of intensity and seasons of rest. You can travel. You can scale back without disappearing. You can say yes only to work that fits your energy and values now, not just your skills.

This does not appear immediately. Early independence often feels more constrained than employment.

That is not freedom from work.

It is freedom in how work happens.

The First Year

Pattern Recognition

Now that you understand the operating model, here is what adjusting to it tends to feel like.

The first year of independence is rarely defined by technical difficulty. The work itself often feels familiar. Systems behave the same. Meetings feel similar. Deliverables look recognizable.

What changes is how uncertainty feels.

There may be a month where calls come easily and confidence rises. There may be a month where nothing moves and doubt surfaces quietly. You may question whether independence was premature even when nothing is structurally wrong.

This fluctuation is normal.

In employment, momentum is institutional. In independence, momentum is personal.

There will likely be:

- The first engagement that ends earlier than expected
- The first proposal that does not convert
- The first slow week that feels heavier than it should
- The first pricing conversation that tests your resolve

None of these mean you are failing. They mean you are operating without institutional buffers.

The first year is not about perfect execution. It is about learning patterns and adjusting expectations.

You begin to see how work arrives, how long pipelines really take, which recruiters follow through, which clients operate cleanly, what kinds of scope drift predictably, and where your boundaries need reinforcement.

Confidence in independence does not come from one large engagement. It comes from experiencing variability without overreacting.

The consultants who struggle most in their first year are rarely the least skilled. They are the ones who interpret normal fluctuation as personal judgment.

It is not. It is structural adjustment.

By the end of the first year, something subtle shifts. You stop reacting to every fluctuation. You recognize patterns earlier. You anticipate drift before it expands. You understand your own tolerance more clearly.

Independence begins to feel less like exposure and more like choice.

The first year is not about proving yourself. It is about stabilizing yourself.

Projects Have Lifecycles. Consulting Does Too

Most professionals working in technology or operations are familiar with project lifecycles.

A system implementation typically moves through phases such as requirements gathering, system design, build configuration, testing, and deployment. These phases describe how a project progresses from idea to completion.

Consulting work intersects with those lifecycles, but it operates on a different rhythm.

Independent consultants are rarely present from the beginning of a project to the end. More often they enter somewhere in the middle. A consultant may be asked to help define a problem that has not yet been framed clearly. In other situations, they are brought in during active delivery, or even later when a project has stalled and needs stabilization or go live support.

As a result, consulting work follows its own cycle.

Instead of participating in a single continuous project from start to finish, independent consultants experience a repeating rhythm of opportunities, engagements, closures, and periods between work. Over time this rhythm becomes the normal operating pattern of independent consulting.

Understanding this distinction is important.

Projects follow implementation phases. Consulting follows engagement cycles. Independent consultants move between the two.

One important detail often goes unspoken. Consultants are rarely present for the entire project lifecycle.

Clients bring in consultants at different moments depending on the situation. Sometimes the work begins at the earliest stage, when a problem is still being defined. Other times a consultant arrives in the middle of an initiative that is already underway. In more difficult situations, a consultant may be asked to step in when progress has stalled or when a project needs stabilization.

Because of this, independent consultants must orient themselves quickly. They are not hired to observe the cycle from the beginning. They are hired to enter wherever the situation currently sits and contribute effectively from that point forward.

That ability to orient quickly and become effective is one of the defining skills of experienced consultants.

In practice, the consulting cycle often looks like this:

Opportunity

A recruiter reaches out. A former colleague calls. A client asks for help. Opportunities usually appear through relationships rather than formal marketing.

Discovery

Before work begins, the consultant must understand the situation: the real problem, decision ownership, constraints, and expectations.

Scope Definition

Discovery becomes a defined engagement. Scope clarifies responsibility, boundaries, deliverables, and pricing.

Delivery

The engagement stabilizes. Work progresses, decisions are made, and the consultant contributes within the defined role.

Expectation Management

As the engagement evolves, expectations shift. Successful consultants monitor that drift and reset alignment early.

Closure

Every engagement eventually ends. Professional closure consolidates trust, documents outcomes, and leaves the client confident about the next phase.

The Gap

Between engagements, the calendar opens. This period can feel uncertain early in a consulting career. Over time, it becomes a normal part of the operating rhythm.

Re-entry

New opportunities appear and the cycle begins again.

In reality, a consultant might enter at any point in this sequence. An engagement may begin during discovery, but just as often it begins during delivery or even during recovery when something has already gone off course.

The consultant's responsibility is not to control where the cycle begins. The responsibility is to recognize where the situation currently sits and become effective quickly.

That ability, orienting fast and contributing with clarity, is one of the defining skills of experienced consultants.

The chapters that follow explore many of these phases in more detail. Understanding the full cycle helps explain why independent consulting rarely feels linear.

It moves in seasons rather than in a straight line.

Chapter Summary

Independent consulting is defined by its operating model, not its marketing language. The tasks may look familiar, but the structure beneath the work is different.

In independence, risk becomes visible, volatility becomes personal, and responsibility concentrates instead of diffusing. Visible risk feels uncomfortable, but it can be managed. Hidden risk simply happens to you.

Once you understand the model, early fluctuation becomes pattern recognition rather than panic.

What Comes Next

Understanding the model is necessary. Operating inside it requires infrastructure.

Independent consultants do not function alone. They rely on relationships, reputation, and professional proximity to generate opportunity and stabilize work.

Chapter 3 explores the professional circle that sustains independent practice: how work actually arrives, how trust compounds, and why independence is never isolation.

Part III
Entering the Consulting Market

How opportunities actually appear, how engagements begin, and how the first weeks stabilize.

Chapter 3
Your Professional Circle

The consultant with the best website often isn't the busiest. The busiest consultant often has no website at all.

This surprises people who are new to independent work. It contradicts the advice that dominates LinkedIn feeds and marketing blogs: build a personal brand, post consistently, optimize your profile, stay visible.

That advice is aimed at markets where clients browse, compare, and buy based on public presence—coaches, fractional executives, productized service providers.

Traditional IT consulting is not that market.

When a client is trying to stabilize an ERP implementation, recover a failing one, or backfill a key position that just opened, they are not searching for thought leaders. They are searching for low risk. Someone they can rely on.

Most consulting work, especially in IT, does not come from visibility. It comes from memory. Someone remembers how you showed up when things were unclear, pressured, or difficult.

That memory produces the next call.

Why Relationships Outperform Marketing in IT Consulting

Many experienced IT professionals are quietly uncomfortable with marketing language. Not because they lack ambition, but because it feels disconnected from how work actually happens.

They did not build their careers by promoting themselves. They built them by solving problems that mattered, staying calm when others panicked, and taking responsibility when outcomes were uncertain. Being told that consulting success now depends on content strategy or personal branding at best feels misaligned and, at worst, is insulting.

The reality is simpler.

In IT consulting and staff augmentation, the cost of failure is high. Systems are critical, timelines are unforgiving, and mistakes are visible. In those conditions, clients are rarely trying to discover someone new. They are trying to select someone safe. Someone with proven experience.

Marketing can reinforce trust once someone is already considering you. It rarely creates trust from scratch.

What creates trust is direct experience, a trusted referral, or visible proof of judgment. A former colleague who knows how you work. A client who has seen you handle something difficult. A body of published writing that shows how you think.

For IT consultants, publishing is not a form of lead generation. It is due diligence material.

A hiring manager who is already leaning toward you often does one final thing before committing. They search your name. If what they find is thoughtful and credible, it validates the recommendation they are about to act on. That mechanism is completely different from content marketing. It is not about reach. It is about reassurance.

This chapter focuses on the core consulting model where engagements are relationship driven, trust thresholds are high, and referral is the dominant channel. Consultants building fractional practices or productized offerings operate with different visibility requirements. Later chapters address that model separately.

For the work most experienced IT professionals step into, the principle holds. Reputation travels through relationships, not campaigns.

Trust is the Primary Currency

Trust in consulting is not abstract. It is situational.

Clients remember how you respond to pressure, how you handle uncertainty, and whether you make the environment clearer or noisier. Long after project details blur, they recall whether working with you reduced risk or increased it.

In consulting, trust is not a soft attribute. It is the primary currency. It forms when:

- You communicate clearly when the stakes are high, not just when conditions are calm
- You set realistic expectations and honor them, even when pressure pushes toward overpromising
- You surface problems early and directly, rather than protecting appearances
- You follow through to real completion, not just visible activity
- You leave systems, decisions, and relationships clearer than you found them

Trust formed in those moments often sits dormant until a situation activates it.

Most IT consulting work is triggered by one of five situations:

- A new system implementation or major upgrade
- A project is struggling
- A key person leaves

- A deadline is approaching
- Leadership needs independent judgment without political friction

When one of those conditions appears, the question is rarely who has the best website.

It is usually: Who do we trust to step into this without making the situation worse?

The Professional Circle is Not a Network

Many people use network to describe what actually functions as a professional circle. The distinction matters.

A network is broad and passive. A professional circle is small and active.

Your professional circle consists of people who:

- Have seen your work firsthand
- Understand your judgment, not just your skills
- Are comfortable attaching their reputation to yours

This circle does not need to be large. It works better when it is not. For most independent consultants, the circle includes:

- Former managers who trusted your judgment
- Senior colleagues who saw you operate under pressure
- Recruiters who understand your real strengths
- Peer consultants who refer selectively because they respect how you work
- Former clients who would hire you again

How the circle evolves

Early in a career, the circle is mostly internal. Colleagues. Managers. A few cross-functional partners who saw your work up close.

Over time, the circle shifts.

In five to ten years of independent work, former clients become your most valuable members. Not because they like you, but because they have evidence. They have lived through an engagement with you and can speak about outcomes. That makes their referral credible.

Recruiters also evolve inside your circle. A recruiter who placed you successfully and watched you deliver becomes different from a recruiter who is simply broadcasting roles. They learn where you fit and when they can safely attach their name to yours.

The circle is not static. It has attrition.

People retire. They move industries. They shift into roles where they no longer hire consultants. Some relationships go dormant naturally. Maintaining your circle is not only about deepening existing relationships. It is noticing which ones have gone quiet and deciding whether to refresh them or let them fade.

Independence requires a living circle, not a frozen list.

Some relationships persist for decades when the pattern of work holds. I still work with a small group of recruiters I first met more than twenty-five years ago. Over time, that circle changes as some retire and new recruiters are introduced through referrals from people already in the network.

Two Circles, Two Functions

Independent consultants operate inside two overlapping circles, each serving a different purpose.

The opportunity circle

This is where work originates. It includes recruiters, former clients, former colleagues, and consulting partners. Its job is simple: surface opportunities.

This circle responds to timing, availability, and relevance. When a need appears, this is how you hear about it.

The support circle

This circle exists to protect you once work begins. It includes accountants, insurance brokers, legal advisors, and a small number of trusted peers who can sanity check decisions.

That peer is often one of the most valuable members of your support circle. The person who says that contract language will turn into scope creep, or that the timeline is fantasy, or that client is trying to buy leadership at a contractor rate.

Many new consultants focus heavily on the opportunity circle and neglect the support circle. That imbalance does not hurt immediately. It shows up later, when tax surprises appear, contracts feel unclear, or decisions carry more risk than expected.

Both circles matter. They serve different roles.

Recruiters: Intermediaries Not Adversaries

Recruiters are often misunderstood.

Some consultants approach these conversations as auditions. Others treat them as necessary evils. Both approaches miss the point.

Recruiters are intermediaries. Their job is to reduce risk on both sides.

A good recruiter is not evaluating whether you are impressive. They are assessing:

- Whether you understand the environment
- Whether you communicate clearly
- Whether you will make the client's life easier, not harder
- Whether placing you strengthens their own credibility
- Whether you are reliable and require minimal oversight

The fastest way to build recruiter trust is not enthusiasm. It is precision.

A recruiter call, done well

Generic response:
Sure, I've worked with that system before. I'm happy to help however needed.

Professional response:
Before I confirm interest, I need to understand the situation and scope. Is this coverage for an implementation or upgrade, system stabilization, or a project recovery? And how much travel is involved?

The second response does three things quietly:

- It signals experience
- It replaces assumptions with clarity
- It protects both you and the recruiter from misalignment

Good recruiters appreciate this. It makes their job easier.

When a recruiter pushes back on reasonable clarifying questions, that is information. If they are uncomfortable with basic scope, hours, location cadence, or client expectations, you should assume those areas will remain unclear after you start.

Precision early prevents pain later.

Do Not Burn Bridges That Feed the Practice

Independent consulting is built on relationships. Those relationships are not abstract. They are specific people who choose to bring you into opportunities, represent you to clients, and attach their credibility to your name.

That makes how you handle commitments visible.

A situation appears more often than most expect. A recruiter brings you an opportunity. You review the situation, express interest, and give the green light to move forward. The recruiter presents you to the client. The client approves. A start date is discussed. The process is moving toward a formal agreement.

Then a second opportunity appears.

It may be better aligned. Higher rate. More interesting work. Better location. More control. Now you are holding two paths, but only one can be taken.

This is where many consultants make a mistake. They treat the first opportunity as informal because the contract has not yet been signed. They step away late in the process, often with minimal explanation, assuming that no real commitment existed.

From a transactional perspective, that may feel accurate. From a relationship perspective, it is not.

The recruiter has already invested effort. They have represented you to their client. They have created an expectation on both sides. In many cases, they have chosen you over other candidates and positioned you as the right fit. When you withdraw at that point, the impact is not neutral. It changes how that recruiter sees you. It influences whether they bring you into future opportunities. In some cases, it closes the door entirely.

I have seen this situation play out more than once. The difference in how it is handled is what separates transactional consultants from those who build long-term practices.

Independent consulting is a small world, especially within specific technologies or platforms. Reputation does not spread through announcements. It spreads through moments like this.

This does not mean you must accept every opportunity once it progresses. It does mean you should be deliberate before signaling commitment. A green light should mean something. If your situation changes, communicate early and directly. Do not delay the conversation or avoid it. The longer you wait, the more damage it creates.

When you handle it well, the relationship often holds. When you do not, it rarely does.

There are also situations where protecting your professional circle requires drawing a clear boundary. I had a recruiter request for references as part of a submission, which is normal. What was not normal was using those references to make a sales pitch for his own company. One of those references called me to let me know. That crosses a line. When you provide access to your professional circle, it is based on trust. If that trust is misused, the right response is simple—do not continue the relationship.

Over time, independent consulting becomes less about finding opportunities and more about being trusted with them. That trust is built slowly, and it is shaped in moments that seem small at the time.

Avoiding Duplicate Submissions

Independent consultants are often introduced to the same client need through multiple paths.

A recruiter calls. A consulting firm reaches out. Another intermediary mentions something that sounds familiar. This is common.

What becomes a problem is being submitted to the same end client multiple times through different firms, sometimes without realizing it.

Duplicate submissions create confusion for the client, damage the intermediary's credibility, and reflect poorly on you even when the overlap is unintentional.

As an independent consultant, the responsibility for avoiding this sits with you.

When the client's name is not disclosed

In many cases, the firm submitting you will not disclose the end client name upfront. This is normal. They are protecting a commercial relationship they originated and protecting against being bypassed.

What matters is not immediate disclosure but a clean process.

A non-circumvention agreement is a professional solution. By signing it, you acknowledge the firm's role in the introduction. In return, you gain the ability to confirm that:

- You are not already submitted to that client
- You will not be submitted through another channel simultaneously

This protects everyone involved: the firm, the client, and your reputation.

Why this is your responsibility

No one else sees the full picture.

Recruiters do not know who else contacted you. Consulting firms do not know what conversations you had last week. Clients only see the confusion when it reaches them.

A simple rule helps: One opportunity. One channel. One time.

If clarity is missing, pause before proceeding.

A professional boundary that works

"I'm happy to move forward. Before we do, I need to confirm I'm not already submitted to the same end client through another firm. If needed, I'm comfortable signing a non-circumvention agreement to make that clean."

That sentence signals professionalism, not resistance. It tells the intermediary you understand how the system works and operate carefully inside it.

Why this matters more than it appears

Being double-submitted rarely costs you an opportunity immediately. What it costs you is quieter:

- Trust with the client
- Confidence from intermediaries
- Reputation as someone who operates cleanly

Those losses compound. Consulting careers are not built on volume. They are built on being seen as a safe pair of hands before the work even begins.

Why Most Work Comes from Familiar Names

Independent consulting does not reward novelty. It rewards reliability.

When a manager recommends you internally, they are spending political capital. When a recruiter submits you, they are attaching their reputation. When a former colleague calls you, they are solving a problem they feel responsible for.

Those decisions are not driven by marketing. They are driven by remembered behavior.

This is why many consultants experience a paradox. They stop chasing work, and more work appears. It is not magic. It is trust density.

Once enough people in your circle know exactly what it feels like to work with you, opportunities begin routing toward you without active searching. They do not need a campaign. They need a name that feels safe to say out loud.

There is also a second layer that most consultants miss.

Every engagement is a trust deposit or withdrawal, not only with the client, but with the person who referred you. When someone puts your name forward, you are carrying their credibility into the room. Doing great work strengthens that relationship. A messy engagement damages it even if the client never complains.

This is one reason experienced consultants protect fit so aggressively. They are protecting the relationship behind the referral, not just the current invoice.

Staying Top of Mind Without Selling Yourself

Staying relevant does not require constant self-promotion. It requires continuity.

Simple, professional touchpoints work because they reactivate memory without forcing attention.

What to do

After an engagement ends, send a short closeout message to the person who hired you. Something like:

"I enjoyed working with your team. If anything comes up as you settle into the next phase, feel free to reach out. I'm always happy to sanity check decisions, even if you do not need formal support."

When you learn something useful, share it with the people it actually applies to. Not a link dump. A sentence of context.

"I saw two functional enhancements to the Forecast module in the next ERP upgrade you may be interested in. If you're interested, I'm happy to share what I have on this."

When you become available, let your recruiters know. Communicate cleanly and professionally.

"I'm wrapping up an engagement in mid-April. If something opens up in May that aligns with my background, I'd be open to a conversation." When someone reaches out, respond promptly and clearly.

Speed does not build trust on its own. Clarity does. But silence erodes trust quickly.

What not to do

Avoid broadcast availability messages.

- Avoid generic open-to-opportunities posts.
- Avoid reaching out only when you need something.
- Avoid forced check-ins that add no value.

You are not reminding people that you exist. You are reminding them what it feels like to work with you.

Rebuilding a circle after a long time in one organization

Many readers will have spent ten or fifteen years inside one company. Their relationships are deep but concentrated. When they go independent, their circle can feel narrow and internally trapped.

That is normal.

In the first year, the goal is not to manufacture a huge network. The goal is to diversify reference points.

Start by reconnecting with people who have seen you operate but now work elsewhere. Former colleagues. Former managers. Cross-functional partners who moved on. These are the easiest bridges into an external circle.

Then build one new layer deliberately. One recruiter who places well in your niche. One peer consultant whose judgment you trust. One former client relationship you maintain after the invoice stops.

Circle expansion is not marketing. It is a professional infrastructure.

Chapter Summary

- Most IT consulting work comes from memory, not marketing.
- Trust forms through specific behavior and activates when conditions create urgency.
- Your professional circle is an operating infrastructure, not a networking exercise.
- Strong professional circles compress uncertainty. Weak ones amplify it.

Opportunity is not random. It is relational.

What Comes Next

Relationships create opportunities. Opportunity creates decision pressure.

When the call comes, the discipline shifts from visibility to evaluation. Speed becomes tempting. Precision becomes critical.

Chapter 4 moves into the moment between interest and commitment: deciding what you are actually agreeing to before you sign.

Chapter 4
From Opportunity to Commitment

Deciding What You Are Actually Agreeing To

Relationships create opportunity.
Opportunity creates decision pressure.

Chapter 3 explained where consulting work actually comes from: trust, proximity, timing, and reputation.

This chapter focuses on what happens after that trust produces an opportunity. Not the idealized version but the real one.

For many experienced IT professionals, this phase feels uncomfortable. You have spent years being rewarded for responsiveness. Saying yes quickly. Adapting on the fly. Absorbing ambiguity. Making things work even when conditions were imperfect.

In corporate environments, those instincts are strengths.

In independent consulting, speed without precision creates problems that surface later, usually after you are already committed.

A scope that felt close enough during a rushed conversation becomes scope creep by week three.

What felt like a minor ambiguity at the beginning becomes operational pressure later.

Availability assumptions that were never spoken turn into evening and weekend work by month two. Terms you skimmed become disagreements about accountability, payment, or responsibility.

None of this happens because someone acted in bad faith. It happens because clarity was traded for momentum.

This chapter exists to help you maintain precision under pressure.

You Are Not Onboarding - You Are Contracting

If you are transitioning from employment into independent work, this phase can feel unfamiliar.

In employment, you are accustomed to:

- Receiving offers rather than negotiating commercial terms
- Signing HR documents rather than reviewing statements of work
- Starting quickly without questioning the scope
- Trusting that the organization structured risk on your behalf

In independent consulting, none of that structure exists unless you create it.

There is no HR department ensuring expectations are reasonable. There is no manager above you to absorb ambiguity. There is no legal team protecting your interests unless you engage one.

This does not mean every engagement is adversarial. It means responsibility is explicit.

You are not onboarding into a role. You are contracting into an operating agreement.

That shift matters.

The Recruiter Call

Clarifying the Situation, Not Selling Yourself

Recruiter-led conversations move quickly by design. Rates are often mentioned early. Context arrives later, if at all.

Your goal in the first call is not to impress. It is to determine whether further conversation is warranted.

A useful mental shift helps here.

Recruiters describe situations, not jobs. Clarify early:

- What problem is driving the request right now?
- Is this backfilling, surge capacity, stabilization, or recovery?
- What triggered the need, and what changed recently?
- Is this tied to an implementation, upgrade, migration, or reorganization?
- What is the expected start date?
- Is this remote, hybrid, or on-site, and if travel is involved, what cadence?
- What is the expected duration, and what usually determines extension?

Follow-up questions that prevent later surprises:

- What specifically broke or changed when the last person left?
- Is the need execution support, advisory judgment, or both?
- Who is the day-to-day owner on the client side?

If the recruiter cannot explain beyond keywords, that is not a failure. It is information.

When the rate question comes too early

It almost always does.

A recruiter asks, what is your rate, before you have any meaningful context. That puts new independents in a trap. Name a number too early, and you price blind. Refuse to answer, and you sound evasive.

A clean approach is to anchor the relationship and request context without dodging:

"I can be flexible depending on scope, work mode, travel expectations, and responsibility. If you can walk me through the situation and expectations, I can give you a number that is accurate instead of a guess."

If they press again, narrow it to a range and tie it to assumptions:

"If this is standard execution support with defined scope and minimal travel, my range is X to Y. If it involves recovery work, significant travel, or outcome accountability, we should align scope and structure first because the rate changes with the risk."

You are not being difficult. You are preventing pricing without understanding.

Chapter 9 goes deeper into rate strategy, but this is the moment where pressure hits first.

Rate, Terms, and Availability

Alignment Before Negotiation

At this stage, the conversation is less about negotiating and more about alignment.

Clarify:

- Bill rate and pay rate if an intermediary is involved
- Engagement structure: Corp-to-Corp, W-2, 1099, or other
- Expected weekly hours
- Overtime expectations and whether it is billable
- After hours or on call expectations
- Timekeeping and approval process

- Payment terms: weekly, net 15, net 30
- Expense and travel reimbursement if applicable
- Any required insurance coverage: general liability, professional liability, cyber, or other
- Any background check, drug screen, or security onboarding requirements that could delay start

Many new consultants hesitate here. They worry that asking commercial questions will make them sound transactional or difficult.

In practice, the opposite is true.

Professional recruiters and clients expect these questions. They signal that you understand how independent work functions. What damages trust is changing the terms after you've verbally committed, being unresponsive, or discovering a major misalignment after you've started.

A useful principle still applies.

If a recruiter reacts negatively to reasonable commercial clarification, that reaction is data about how the engagement will likely unfold.

The Client Conversation

What You Are Really Assessing

Client interviews are rarely formal interviews. They are fit and confident conversations.

Clients are evaluating whether:

- You understand their environment quickly.
- You have knowledge of specific system functions.
- You ask the right questions.
- You remain steady under pressure.
- You communicate clearly without posturing.

You are evaluating something different. You are listening for:

- Clarity versus chaos: can they explain the situation coherently?
- Ownership versus vacuum: is there a real decision maker?
- Realism versus wishful thinking: do timelines match reality?
- Collaboration versus desperation: do they want a partner or a scapegoat?
- Technical problem versus organizational dysfunction.

None of these is an automatic deal breaker. However, you should enter knowing which pattern you are stepping into.

Strong diagnostic questions include:

- What does success look like in the first 30 days?
- What happens if this does not improve?
- Who sets priorities and approves changes?
- What has already been tried, and what failed?

Clients rarely expect immediate answers. They are watching how you think.

When the client describes something different than the recruiter did

This is common.

The recruiter says stabilization. The client describes a recovery effort. The recruiter says advisory support. The client expects full-time ownership. The recruiter says short-term. The client suggests a long-term systems rollout.

Do not argue in the moment. Do not pretend it is fine. Name the mismatch calmly and pull clarity into it.

"Based on what you just described, this sounds broader than stabilization. Before we move forward, I want to make sure scope and expectations are aligned across everyone involved so there are no surprises after day one."

Then follow up with an email to the recruiter or account manager with the specific delta. Not emotion. Facts.

When the Client Says Yes

Do Not Relax, Get Precise

Once a client signals intent, everything accelerates. You may hear:

- They liked you
- Paperwork is coming today
- They want you to start on Monday

This is not the moment to relax; it is the time to become precise.

Paperwork often feels routine. It is not.

Contracts and statements of work are written to contain risk, not to create operational clarity. Many are drafted from templates before anyone speaks with you. They can describe a generic role that does not match what was actually discussed.

Your job is to close that gap before you sign.

The Statement of Work Is the Center of Gravity

Recruiters may refer to the consulting agreement as the contract. In practice:

- The master agreement governs the relationship.
- The statement of work governs the work.

This is where scope, responsibility, assumptions, and exclusions live.

If the SOW is inadequate, you have three options:

1. Request revision with specific language
2. Document your interpretation and ask for written confirmation
3. Decline the engagement

Signing and hoping for clarity to emerge later is not optimism. It is risk deferral.

Option Two

What Documenting Your Understanding Looks Like

This can be simple. Usually, it is just an email.

A clean version sounds like this:

"Based on our conversations, here is my understanding of the role and scope. I will focus on X and Y. This engagement excludes Z unless we add it explicitly. Standard availability is business hours in the agreed upon time zone. After-hours support is limited to true production incidents. The engagement will include limited travel, approximately three to four site visits. Please confirm this aligns with your expectations before I begin."

That message does two things:

- It creates shared memory.
- It makes the scope drift visible when expectations begin to change.

What to Verify Before You Sign

If time is compressed and you can only verify a few things, prioritize these.

Role and scope alignment

Ensure the SOW reflects what was discussed: responsibilities, environment, duration, and work mode.

Responsibility boundaries

Watch for language that assigns ownership of outcomes without authority.

Problematic:

- Consultant will ensure successful project delivery

Clearer:

- Consultant will provide expertise and recommendations to support project success

If you are expected to own outcomes, the agreement must also grant authority, access, decision rights, and a structure that makes ownership real. If it does not, you are signing into a mismatch.

Assumptions and exclusions

Strong SOWs state what is not included.

For example, This engagement excludes training, project management, and on-call rotation unless explicitly added.

This is not being difficult; it is being precise.

Availability expectations

Confirm hours, time zone, response expectations, and after-hours language explicitly.

Commercial mechanics

How you are paid is not an administrative detail. It reveals how responsibility, scope, and risk are structured.

If you do not understand the payment terms, you likely do not understand the expectations attached to them.

Also, confirm where you sit in the subcontracting chain. Are you contracting directly with the end client, or through one firm, or through multiple layers? Each layer can affect communication clarity, payment timing, and who can actually approve scope changes.

Ownership, work product, and IP

Many consulting services agreements contain broad ownership language that assigns all work product to the client or intermediary, sometimes regardless of when it was created or how it is later reused.

If you bring reusable tools, scripts, templates, reports, or custom system enhancements into an engagement, that language can unintentionally transfer rights you never intended to give up.

Non-compete, exclusivity, and competitor restrictions

These clauses are increasingly common. Some agreements restrict you from working with client competitors during the engagement, or for a period afterwards. Others require exclusivity, which makes it difficult to maintain the pipeline. Even when these clauses are framed as standard, they can materially change your ability to operate independently. Review them carefully and clarify what they mean in practice.

In some cases, you may already have existing relationships in the same industry, including former clients or ongoing engagements. When that is true, it is important to clarify those relationships and adjust the agreement's language so that legitimate prior work or existing clients are not unintentionally restricted.

Insurance and onboarding delays

Enterprise clients may require specific insurance and background checks or security onboarding, which can take time.

If a client says start Monday, but onboarding takes two weeks, you need clarity on what happens during that gap. Is there paid prep work? Do you delay the start date? Do you absorb the idle time?

These details affect cash flow and scheduling more than new consultants expect.

Recruiters or agencies may push back on proposed revisions. That is expected. Their role is to manage risk for their client and their firm, just as your responsibility is to manage risk for yourself.

When reasonable clarifications are accepted, you proceed cleanly. When they are not, that resistance is information about how the engagement is likely to operate once you begin.

This is not a signal to argue or escalate. It is a signal to slow down.

Get a lawyer to review what you are signing, especially when the agreement covers ownership, IP, liability, or outcome responsibility.

Move Fast Without Moving Blind

Early engagements often arrive with urgency. A client needs coverage quickly. A project is behind. A recruiter is trying to secure a resource before someone else does.

Speed is often real. So is risk.

Independent consulting requires you to operate in both directions at once. You must respond promptly without surrendering clarity. You can respect urgency without abandoning review. You can move quickly without agreeing blindly.

Professionalism does not mean hesitation. It means precision under pressure.

What this sounds like:

- I can accommodate Monday, but I need to review the SOW carefully first
- This section is ambiguous about after-hours support. Can we clarify in writing before I sign?
- The role description implies leadership responsibility that we did not discuss. I am open to a revised scope or rate alignment, but I cannot sign it as written

This is not a delay. This is professionalism.

Common Risk Patterns

Not Paranoia

Most consulting engagements are not adversarial. They are imperfect.

Clients move quickly. Priorities shift. Language gets drafted before roles are fully clarified. Expectations evolve under pressure. None of this is malicious. Much of it is structural.

Over time, certain patterns repeat.

Execution role with outcome accountability

You are hired to execute but expected to own results controlled by others.

It often sounds like:

- Just take ownership of this.
- We need you to make it happen.
- You are the expert, so you are accountable.

If you do not have authority over resourcing, decision making, priorities, or change control, outcome ownership is not real. It is a liability.

Name the mismatch early. Reframe accountability in terms of influence:

I can own analysis, recommendations, and execution within my control. Final outcomes depend on decisions and resources owned by the client. Let's make those decision points explicit.

Scope as a placeholder for panic

The SOW is vague because the client does not actually know what they need. They are hoping clarity will emerge once you start.

It often appears as:

- Provide technical expertise for optimization.
- Support the team as needed.

- Assist with system improvements.

That language is not in scope. It is anxiety.

How to respond without being bureaucratic:

- Propose an initial scoping window and a checkpoint.

  "For the first two weeks I will assess the environment, confirm priorities, and produce a short scope and plan. At that point, we can lock phase one deliverables and adjust the SOW if needed."

This turns vague need into structured work.

Availability expansion

Small exceptions accumulate into permanent expectations.

A quick response becomes a habit. A one-time after hours assist becomes an assumption. A favor becomes precedent.

Prevent it in week one by naming the boundary calmly:

My standard availability is business hours. After hours support is limited to true production incidents. If recurring off-hours work becomes necessary, we should align scope and structure explicitly.

None of these patterns is fatal. All require early naming.

A Situation You Cannot Always See Coming

Even when you ask good questions before accepting an engagement, you cannot always see the full situation until you are inside the project.

Early in my career as an independent consultant, I received a call from a consulting firm looking for an ERP manufacturing contractor. They needed someone to step into a project where another consultant had recently left.

That detail immediately raised the question: Why did the previous consultant leave?

The explanation I received was vague. The firm described the assignment as a short engagement to provide training on manufacturing accounting and product costing. They also mentioned that the work will expand into a larger system upgrade.

The second phase made the opportunity attractive.

I was aware there were data issues in the environment and that a technical team was working to resolve them. Still, the explanation about the previous consultant's departure felt incomplete.

I chose to move forward.

The engagement was remote. During my first week, I delivered training on the ERP system's manufacturing accounting and product costing functionality to members of the finance team.

Shortly after the training concluded, I received an email from the Plant Director asking me to sign documentation related to financial records for an ongoing audit. He was clearly under pressure and trying to move the audit forward quickly.

The request immediately raised a boundary issue.

My role was to provide system training and functional guidance on manufacturing accounting within the ERP system. I was not a financial auditor, and I did not have the authority to sign documentation related to a company's financial records.

I responded that I could assist with explaining how the system produced costing data, but I could not sign audit documentation on behalf of their organization. The situation escalated quickly. The Plant Director contacted the consulting firm that had placed me, expressing frustration and even threatening to end their relationship.

At that point, it became clear that the environment I had entered was far more unstable than originally described.

Situations like this reinforce an important principle of independent consulting.

You cannot always control the conditions you enter. But you must always take responsibility for what you accept.

Signing financial audit documentation would have created exposure far beyond the scope of the engagement.

Another lesson came from that experience as well. In situations like this, it is often better to involve the consulting firm or intermediary immediately and allow them to manage the issue with the client. They are part of the engagement structure and can help reset expectations at the organizational level.

Early in my independent career, I handled the response directly. With more experience, I learned that involving the intermediary early can prevent unnecessary escalation and protect the relationship on all sides.

Years later, I happened to work on another project with the consultant I had originally replaced on that assignment. During a conversation about past projects, he explained that he had left that engagement due to the same situation. The environment had become difficult due to pressure from the same director.

That conversation confirmed something many independent consultants eventually learn.

When a project begins with warning signals, those signals often reflect deeper organizational dynamics rather than a temporary misunderstanding. Recognizing those patterns early becomes an important professional skill.

When to Say No

Independence expands your options. It also expands your exposure.

In employment, misalignment can be absorbed. Roles evolve. Assignments shift. Teams rotate.

In independence, every yes is deliberate. Every engagement shapes your calendar, your energy, and your reputation.

That is why saying no becomes a professional skill.

Saying no is difficult, especially when the pipeline feels uncertain. The financial pressure is real. In early independence, turning down paying work can feel like turning down safety.

But accepting misaligned work carries costs that are harder to see in the moment:

- Burnout.
- Reputation risk.
- Opportunity cost.
- And calendar saturation that prevents better aligned work from reaching you.

Predictable costs of misalignment:

- It consumes time and capacity that could be reserved for better aligned engagements
- It creates stress you cannot resolve because authority and responsibility are mismatched

- It erodes professional integrity as you absorb expectations you never agreed to own
- It strains relationships when expectations eventually collide

Professional exits sound calm:

- This does not align with my current focus
- The scope is broader than discussed
- I cannot commit to this timeline, but I may be available later

Boundaries do not damage good relationships. They prevent bad engagements.

I once received a call from a project manager leading an ERP implementation in Central America. He told me I was exactly the profile he needed for his resource needs.

The structure sounded impressive. International site. High visibility. Eight-month engagement.

Then he explained the cadence. Three weeks on site. Seven days a week. Ten-hour days. Living on a secure compound. One week home. Then repeat.

I had seen that pattern before.

The compensation was strong. The need was real. But the structure did not align with how I wanted to work or live.

I declined. Not because it was difficult, it was misaligned.

Eight months of intensity can be manageable. Six months of structural misalignment compounds quickly. Burnout rarely arrives dramatically. It accumulates.

Saying no protected my capacity for better-aligned work that followed.

Chapter Summary

Opportunity feels energizing. Commitment creates consequences.

Independent consultants do not onboard. They contract. That shift demands precision in recruiter calls, client conversations, and paperwork review.

Speed creates pressure. Clarity prevents misalignment. Precision under pressure is not hesitation. It is professionalism.

What Comes Next

Signing well protects the front door.

But even well-structured agreements can drift if the engagement begins without rhythm. Clarity on paper does not guarantee stability in practice.

Chapter 5 moves inside the first week of real work and shows how operating rhythm is established before urgency defines it.

Chapter 5
Week One: Establishing the Operating Rhythm

Opening

Engagements do not stabilize on their own. They stabilize because someone shapes them early.

Start dates move quickly. Clarity rarely does.

In independent consulting, the work often begins before alignment does. Access arrives in pieces. Stakeholders are busy. Systems are only partially documented. Ownership is assumed rather than stated. Expectations exist, but they live in people's heads, not in shared language.

Week one is where this either gets corrected or quietly locked in.

The first week does not determine technical success. It determines operating rhythm. It sets communication cadence. It establishes how ambiguity will be handled. It signals whether urgency will drive decisions or whether structure will.

Small choices early create long consequences later. When structure is established intentionally, engagements tend to stabilize. When it is not, urgency becomes the operating system and everything that follows is reactive.

The Purpose of Week One

Week one is not about output. It is about alignment.

Your primary objectives are to:

- Secure systems access, if applicable.
- Confirm how work enters your queue.
- Identify key contacts and who owns decisions and priorities.
- Clarify what success looks like in the first few weeks.
- Establish communication cadence and tone.
- Identify meetings relevant to your scope of work.
- Make availability expectations real rather than theoretical.
- Document assumptions and dependencies.
- Clarify how progress should be communicated.

Experienced consultants know this instinctively. New consultants often skip it, usually because nothing appears wrong yet.

The absence of friction in week one does not mean alignment exists. It usually means misalignment has not surfaced.

The difference between a clean start and a fragile one is whether alignment is made explicit.

The week one written artifact

A simple written artifact at the end of week one helps create shared memory. This may take the form of:

- A brief alignment note
- A written summary of priorities and ownership
- A recap of what you understand as the scope and expectations

The goal is not reporting for its own sake. The goal is shared memory and documented alignment.

Mechanically, keep it simple:

- Send it as a short email to the client stakeholder who owns your priorities
- If a recruiter, account manager, or intermediary is involved, copy them
- If the client prefers a shared document, paste the same note into that space and reference it by date

When alignment is documented early, future corrections feel like refinement rather than rework.

Establishing Structure Without Sounding Bureaucratic

Many consultants worry that early alignment conversations make them sound procedural or heavy-handed.

In most environments, professional clients expect early clarity. In some fast-moving cultures, they may not expect it, and they may react with impatience. That does not mean the questions are wrong. It means your framing matters.

A practical framing is results first:

- "I want to make sure I focus on the right things from day one so you see progress quickly."
- "Before I start, can you walk me through the service ticket process from submission to resolution?"
- "Based on our discussion, here is what I understand so far. If anything is off, I want to correct it now."

These are clarity exercises. They are not governance exercises.

The Two Conversations That Matter Most

Most early instability in consulting engagements is not technical. It is conversational.

Work begins before assumptions are surfaced. Tasks move before priorities are clarified. Requests arrive before ownership is defined. Everyone assumes alignment exists because no one has yet named misalignment.

Two early conversations prevent most drift. They do not require authority. They require initiative.

Scheduled intentionally in the first week, these conversations establish an operating rhythm. Without them, urgency fills the vacuum.

1. The Priority and Success Conversation

This conversation answers one question: what matters first. Useful prompts include:

- What would make this engagement a success in the first 30 days?
- What is most urgent right now, and why?
- Who are my key contacts for this initiative, and what decisions does each person own?
- What should not be touched until we align?
- What does "done" look like for the first phase?

This conversation prevents a common failure: being productive on the wrong things.

2. The Ownership and Flow Conversation

This conversation answers a different question: how decisions actually happen. Clarify:

- Who approves priorities and scope changes?
- How requests should enter: email, ticketing, meetings, teams?
- What the escalation path is for issues?
- What change of control looks like in practice?

- How you should communicate progress: brief emails, a standing meeting, a shared tracker, or a weekly recap.

Without this conversation, consultants often become the default owner of everything, not because anyone intended it, but because no one named the alternative.

Reading the Room in Week One

Every organization has unwritten norms. Some live in email. Some live in Teams. Some live in hallway conversations. Some expect formal meeting invites for everything. Others expect you to join existing calls without ceremony.

Week one is when you learn:

- Where real decisions are made
- Whether people prefer concise summaries or live discussion
- What tone is considered professional in that environment
- How quickly leadership expects updates, and in what format

Getting these norms wrong rarely causes immediate conflict. It creates subtle friction that is hard to diagnose later. Learn the norms early and match them.

Working Alongside Other Consultants or Contractors

Many engagements include multiple external resources. If you do not clarify intersections early, you can end up duplicating effort or stepping on ownership without realizing it.

In week one, confirm:

- Who else is engaged externally, and what their scope is
- Where your scope overlaps, and who owns decisions in the overlap
- Whether there is a shared work tracker or handoff process

- Whether the client expects you to coordinate directly with the other resources

When roles are unclear, turf conflict shows up as "communication issues." Prevent it early by naming roles and boundaries.

Making Availability Real

Availability is often assumed rather than defined.

Most contracts include language about business hours or support expectations. But written language and lived behavior are not the same thing. In the absence of explicit reinforcement, availability quietly expands.

A quick response becomes a habit. A one-time after hours assist becomes an expectation. A favor becomes precedent.

Even if the availability language exists in the contract, week one is where it becomes real.

Clarify:

- Business hours and time zone expectations
- What constitutes a true production incident
- How after-hours requests should be handled
- Whether recurring off-hours work is expected

A simple statement early prevents resentment later:

"My standard availability is during business hours. After hours support is for true production incidents. If recurring off-hours work becomes necessary, we should align expectations and scope explicitly."

One nuance matters more than most people realize: your first enforcement moment defines the boundary.

You can state the boundary in week one, but if you respond to a non-emergency message at 9 PM in week two, you have reset expectations regardless of what you said. Verbal boundaries become real only when behavior matches them.

Documenting Assumptions and Dependencies

Consulting engagements rarely begin with full clarity. They begin with movement.

Work starts while system access is still pending. Meetings are scheduled before documentation is reviewed. Decisions are referenced before they are formally recorded. Everyone operates on shared expectations that have never been written down.

Assumptions fill the gaps. Common assumptions include:

- Access will be granted quickly
- Data is reliable
- Environments match documentation
- Stakeholders will be available
- Decisions will be made on time

Most assumptions are reasonable. The problem is not that they exist. The problem is that they remain implicit.

When assumptions remain unspoken, delays quietly become personal. Gaps become blame.

A summary message changes the dynamic. Include:

- What you are assuming
- What you need to proceed
- What you are starting with
- What success looks like for the first phase
- A short risks and dependencies list

Not a formal risk register. Just a simple statement of reality:

"These items must happen for this timeline to hold."

That converts a future argument into a reference point.

Documentation Protects Both Sides

Occasionally, a client will push for speed and suggest skipping documentation.

Early in one engagement, a Director of IT told me directly not to spend time documenting the system design. His view was simple: do not waste time writing documents, just implement the system.

I understood the urgency behind the request. Projects often feel time-sensitive, and documentation can appear to slow progress in the moment.

But I did not change my approach.

As an independent consultant, system design and configuration documentation is not optional. It protects both the consultant and the client.

In fact, professional liability insurance policies often require consultants to maintain reasonable documentation of system design decisions, configuration changes, and project work. Those records demonstrate how decisions were made and provide a reference if questions arise later.

Documentation records how the system was structured, what decisions were made, and how the configuration was implemented. Even when clients are focused on speed, disciplined documentation remains part of the work.

I continued documenting the system design and configuration as the implementation progressed.

About three months after the engagement ended, the consulting firm that had placed me on the project called. The client was asking them for the design documentation from the implementation.

Because the documentation had been produced during the engagement, the consulting firm was able to provide exactly what the client needed.

Situations like this reinforce a simple consulting reality.

Projects move quickly. Personnel change. New questions emerge long after the implementation work is complete.

Documentation becomes the institutional memory of the project. Producing it protects everyone involved.

Administrative Readiness: Reducing Friction When It Counts

Momentum is fragile in the early days of an engagement. Many engagements stall not because of scope disagreement, but because paperwork lags.

Administrative readiness is not clerical. It is professional preparedness.

Common items to have ready:

- W-9
- Business registration details
- ACH banking information
- Certificate of insurance, if required
- Background check information, if required
- A one-page capability summary for recruiter submissions

Insurance becomes normal operating overhead in independent work. It protects you from risks of employment once absorbed.

Most commonly requested types include:

- General liability, basic business coverage
- Professional liability, often called errors and omissions coverage
- Cyber liability, sometimes required for access to sensitive systems

Chapter 6 covers structure in more detail. Here, the point is simple: do not let insurance or onboarding paperwork become the reason you miss a clean start.

The one-page capability summary

Keep it simple and reusable. Include:

- Your name and company name
- Role and core capabilities in one sentence
- Two to four relevant experience bullets tied to outcomes
- Systems or platforms you specialize in
- Work mode and travel preferences
- Availability window
- Contact information

This is not marketing. It is a clean submission aid.

The Handoff: Recruiter to Client

There is often an awkward transition where the recruiter who managed the pre-engagement relationship steps back, and you are now operating directly with the client.

Clarify in week one:

- Who your commercial contact is for terms and changes
- Who your operational contact is for priorities and workflow
- Whether the recruiter or account manager wants to be copied on status or only on issues
- What to do if misalignment emerges and you need escalation

If something goes wrong later, you do not want to be deciding in real time which direction to point the problem.

When Misalignment Emerges Anyway

Early structure reduces risk. It does not eliminate it.

Even when you do everything right, misalignment can still emerge:

- Key stakeholders were not involved in scoping
- The problem is larger than initially understood
- Organizational dynamics apply pressure to the contract that was never anticipated

Address it early. Effective responses include:

- Documenting what you are seeing in specific terms
- Proposing options rather than complaints
- Involving the recruiter or account manager if appropriate
- Knowing your exit criteria before resentment builds

Silently absorbing an expanded scope is not professionalism. It is deferred failure.

There was a time when I was brought in to manage an ERP project. The Statement of Work outlined project management responsibilities, governance checkpoints, and reporting expectations. It was reasonable to assume the project had received steering committee approval before external leadership was engaged.

Two months into the engagement, I discovered it had not. The work stopped immediately.

No amount of competent delivery can compensate for a structural failure of sponsorship.

Once that gap surfaces, momentum disappears.

What matters is recognizing the signals early. Stakeholder gaps. Sponsors who hesitate when decisions require formal backing. Escalations that feel disproportionate to the stated scope. Those are the moments to ask direct questions, not after three months of execution.

Exit criteria do not need to be dramatic. It can be simple: if the scope expands beyond what was contracted and the client will not renegotiate after a direct conversation, that is an exit signal.

What a Well Structured Engagement Looks Like

It is important to say this clearly: not every engagement is fragile.

When early alignment is intentional, when scope is named, and when ownership is clarified, consulting work stabilizes quickly. The environment feels purposeful rather than reactive. Energy goes toward execution instead of interpretation.

A well-structured engagement does not feel dramatic. It feels calm.

A manufacturing client needs ERP support after a key person leaves. The recruiter explains the situation clearly. The SOW matches the conversation. The client confirms priorities and ownership. Access is ready. Communication is professional.

By week three:

- The scope is stable
- Availability expectations are respected
- Progress is visible
- Stress remains contained

These engagements are not rare. They are the result of intentional early structure.

Chapter Summary

Most consulting instability is not caused by incompetence. It is caused by ambiguity that no one named early enough.

The first week is not ceremonial. It is foundational.

Week one is where the operating rhythm gets set. Priorities, ownership, request flow, communication cadence, availability, and assumptions either become explicit or they become silent liabilities. When structure is established intentionally, engagements stabilize. When it is not, urgency becomes the operating system.

What Comes Next

Stabilizing one engagement is tactical. Sustaining independence requires clarity across engagements.

Before pricing, scaling, or long-term positioning, you must be able to define precisely what responsibilities you carry and where they end.

Chapter 6 moves from engagement mechanics to service definition.

Part IV
Structuring the Practice

Defining what you offer, building the minimum infrastructure, and understanding the rhythm of independent work.

Chapter 6 — Defining Your Service

Chapter 7 — The Minimum Viable Structure

Chapter 8 — A Day in the Life of an Independent Consultant

Chapter 6
Defining Your Service

By this point, you have seen how independent consulting actually begins. Work appears through trust rather than marketing. Commitments form under pressure. Week one determines whether an engagement stabilizes or drifts.

All of that only works if you can do one thing clearly:

You must be able to explain what you take responsibility for and, just as importantly, what you do not.

Most experienced IT professionals assume their résumé is the answer: the systems they have worked on, the roles they have held, the years they have accumulated. Clients may listen politely and still not know what they are buying.

This chapter exists to close that gap.

Why Experience Is Not a Service

After the structure is established, a deeper question remains: what are you actually being hired to do?

Clients do not hire experience in the abstract. They hire relief.

Something is not working. Something feels risky. Something is falling behind. A system is unstable, a project is stalled, or a key person is gone. The client does not want to admire your background. They want the situation to improve.

When consultants define their service in résumé language, several things happen quietly:

- Conversations drift toward tasks instead of outcomes
- Pricing becomes anchored to time rather than responsibility
- Scope expands because no one stated where it ends
- Clients assign ownership without realizing they are doing it

None of this is malicious. It is structural.

If you cannot articulate your service clearly, the client will define it for you, usually in ways that increase responsibility without increasing clarity.

The TRI Framework

I refer to this simple structure as the TRI framework: Trigger, Responsibility, Impact.

In simple terms,

- The trigger explains why the client called.
- Responsibility defines what you agree to carry.
- Impact describes what becomes different because you were involved.

Service definition has three elements:

- Trigger
- Responsibility
- Impact

This chapter gives you a practical way to define your service using those three elements.

TRI is not branding. It is an operating discipline. It moves conversations out of biography and into business reality.

A clean service definition can often be stated in two to three sentences.

It should contain all three elements. When it does, recruiter calls improve, scope stays cleaner, and pricing conversations become more grounded.

Now we build it.

Trigger

Every consulting engagement begins with a trigger. Something changes and internal capacity no longer feels sufficient.

Many triggers are urgent:

- A new system implementation or major upgrade
- A system failure
- A missed milestone
- A key person leaves
- A looming deadline
- Post go-live instability

But not all triggers are crises. Some are strategic:

- Leadership is considering a major system change and wants experienced judgment before committing
- A program is active but stuck, and leadership wants clarity before investing more
- A decision feels high risk, and the organization wants an independent perspective without internal politics

Clients rarely say: "We wanted someone with fifteen years of experience."

They say:

- "We're falling behind."
- "One of our key IT people moved on in the middle of an ERP implementation."
- "We're dealing with instability and nobody can explain why."
- "We don't know what to do next."

- "We need someone who can dig in and get this back under control."

Service definition starts there, not with you.

Responsibility

If the trigger explains why you were called, responsibility defines what you are actually being paid to carry.

Responsibility is not task execution. It is what you agree to own when the instructions are incomplete.

Two consultants can do similar work and carry very different responsibilities. Example:

- Consultant A runs the month-end close exactly as documented. They execute steps and report results.
- Consultant B runs the month-end close, but also identifies why it keeps breaking, surfaces cross functional bottlenecks, challenges assumptions that are no longer true, and recommends changes that prevent recurrence.

Same system. Same month. Completely different responsibility profile.

Common forms of responsibility in independent IT work include:

Diagnosing the real problem

Not the ticket description. Not the symptom. The actual cause.

This often includes separating process breakdown from system defect, and separating data quality from configuration.

Sequencing what matters first

You decide what gets stabilized first, what can wait, and what should not be touched yet.

You protect the client from doing the wrong work quickly.

Reducing risk through judgment

You choose safer paths when the environment is unclear.

You know when a change is reversible and when it is not.

Absorbing ambiguity so others do not have to

You hold uncertainty and translate it into next steps.

You reduce emotional noise in environments where everyone feels behind.

Making progress visible when the situation is messy

You create a clear narrative of what changed, what is still unknown, and what is needed next.

This is where trust is built. Not in activity, but in clarity.

Many consultants underprice themselves because they describe tasks. Clients are paying for responsibility.

Impact

If responsibility defines what you carry, impact defines what changes.

Impact is not effort. It is what becomes different because you were involved.

Clients rarely remember everything you did. They remember how things felt after you arrived.

Impact often shows up as:

- Escalations stop
- Decisions move
- Systems stabilize
- Planning becomes reliable again
- Teams regain confidence
- Work becomes executable again

- Leadership can see the path forward

Impact is how clients recognize value. It is also how they decide whether to extend, refer, or rehire.

Two Legitimate Consulting Models

Most independent IT consultants operate in one or both of these models. The difference is not hierarchy. It is orientation.

Specialist work

The trigger is usually operational pressure. Something is unstable or time-critical.

The responsibility is execution plus diagnosis, often under live conditions.

The impact is continuity. The business continues to operate while underlying issues are addressed.

Advisory work

The trigger is usually complexity and stalled movement. The organization has activity, but not progress.

The responsibility is judgment. You surface decision bottlenecks, clarify ownership, and reset sequencing.

The impact is clarity and momentum. Leadership can make informed decisions and execution becomes possible again.

Many careers include both. What matters is naming which one you are carrying in a given engagement, because pricing, scope, and sustainability change when the model changes.

Why Project Management Skills Matter

Many successful independent IT consultants eventually develop a secondary capability that significantly increases their effectiveness: practical project management.

Even when a consultant is hired for technical expertise, projects rarely succeed through technical knowledge alone. Progress depends on coordination, communication, and structured execution.

Someone must clarify priorities, track decisions, manage dependencies, and maintain momentum when multiple stakeholders are involved.

In well-run organizations, this role is handled by a formal project manager. In many environments, however, the consultant becomes the person who quietly introduces structure.

This does not necessarily mean the consultant becomes the official project manager. It means they bring project management discipline into the engagement.

Practical examples include:

- Organizing requirements discussions into clear decisions
- Documenting design choices and configuration assumptions
- Tracking action items and ownership
- Clarifying dependencies between teams
- Communicating progress in a way stakeholders can understand

These behaviors are often what differentiate an effective consultant from a purely technical resource.

For professionals considering independent consulting, developing familiarity with basic project management practices can significantly increase both effectiveness and opportunity. The combination of technical depth and operational structure is often where consultants provide the most value.

Field Example: When Technical Work Expands into Project Leadership

In several engagements I have been brought in to perform very specific ERP-related work. The scope might involve system configuration, manufacturing planning, product costing, or other functional areas.

Once the work begins and the client becomes comfortable with your ability to analyze problems and communicate clearly, something interesting often happens.

Additional responsibility starts to appear.

I have had situations where a client originally brought me in for technical ERP tasks and then asked me to help coordinate a series of special projects that were struggling to move forward.

The technical work opened the door. The need for structure created the opportunity.

In those cases, my role expanded beyond system configuration into helping organize project work. That might involve structuring meetings, clarifying objectives, tracking decisions, and helping different departments stay aligned on priorities.

These were not always formal project management assignments. In many cases, the organization simply needed someone who could introduce structure and keep initiatives moving.

Over time, I found myself providing guidance on project management approaches for clients quite often, even though the original engagement was technical.

This pattern appears frequently in consulting work.

Clients initially hire experts for a specific problem. As trust develops, they often rely on the consultant to bring structure to broader initiatives that lack clear coordination.

For consultants who are comfortable operating in both technical and organizational spaces, this can become an important source of additional value.

TRI in Practice

Below are two service definitions. Each contains a trigger, responsibility, and impact.

Specialist example

Trigger: critical operations are under pressure, such as month-end close failures, MRP instability, production disruptions, or post go-live chaos.

Responsibility: I diagnose what is actually broken, stabilize workflows, and manage changes carefully so fixes do not create new failures.

Impact: operations regain reliability quickly so the business can keep shipping while deeper root causes are addressed.

Advisory example

Trigger: complex IT initiatives stall despite heavy activity, unclear ownership, or repeated rework.

Responsibility: I surface bottlenecks, clarify decision ownership, reset sequencing, and help leadership see what is blocking execution.

Impact: decision making becomes cleaner, priorities become executable, and delivery regains momentum without political friction.

Where Staff Augmentation Fits

Many independents enter through contract or staff augmentation roles. That structure is common and legitimate.

Staff augmentation describes how you are engaged. It does not define what you carry.

In staff augmentation roles:

- You may be embedded within an existing team
- Work is often assigned rather than defined
- Pricing is typically time-based
- Reporting lines may resemble employment more than consulting

Some of these engagements remain narrowly execution focused. Others evolve.

You will know responsibility is shifting when you start hearing:

- "What do you think we should do?"
- "If you were in my seat, would you….?"
- "Can you lead this and get alignment?"

That shift is not a problem. It is a signal.

When responsibility expands, scope and expectations must expand with it. If the engagement stays priced and structured like coverage, but you are being asked to carry outcomes, burnout and pricing pressure follow quietly.

Defining Your Service in Client Language

Internal clarity is necessary. External clarity is what clients experience.

Client language describes the problem being solved and the outcome being delivered. It does not lead with credentials.

A clean test:
If a client were explaining to a colleague why they hired me, what would they say?

Rarely:
"They had impressive credentials."

More often:

- "They implemented system modules."
- "They stabilized things."
- "They brought clarity."
- "They helped us avoid expensive mistakes."
- "They made the work executable again."

That is the service.

A Worked Example

Résumé style:
"I'm an ERP manufacturing systems consultant with experience across planning, production, and distribution. I do upgrades, integrations, and support."

Client language using TRI:
"When manufacturing and planning systems need to be implemented, upgraded, or stabilized, clients bring me in to restore clarity and momentum. That may involve launching a new ERP capability, upgrading an existing platform, or stepping in when operations become unstable, planning failures, production disruptions, or the sudden loss of a key resource. My

role is to identify what is actually broken and establish a reliable operating rhythm so the business can keep shipping while the underlying issues are addressed."

Same experience.

Completely different signal.

Pricing Follows Definition

How you define your service determines how you can price it.

If your service is defined as an activity, pricing gets anchored to time:

How many hours, how many weeks, how many tasks?

If your service is defined as responsibility and impact, pricing becomes contextual:

- The risk profile is clearer
- The urgency is clearer
- The level of ownership is clearer
- The cost of delay becomes more visible

Even if the billing unit remains hourly, the rate conversation changes. You are not selling hours. You are selling what you are willing to carry and what improves because you are there.

Chapter 9 builds the full pricing model. This chapter makes pricing possible.

A Simple Exercise That Actually Works

Most experienced consultants already know what they are good at. What they often lack is language that makes it obvious to someone else.

Look back at your last five to seven engagements.

Write three short lists:

- What triggered the call
- What responsibility did you actually carry?
- What changed because you were there

You are not looking for variety. You are looking for repetition.

Then write your service definition in two to three sentences using TRI:

- Trigger
- Responsibility
- Impact

Do not try to be broad. Try to be accurate.

The pattern that appears is not something new. It is the work you have already been doing.

Chapter Summary

Many consultants describe what they can do. Fewer define what they are willing to carry.

Clients do not hire experience in the abstract. They hire relief. A system needs to be implemented, or is unstable, a project is stalled, or a key resource is gone. Defining your service clearly requires naming three elements. The trigger that brings the client to you. The responsibility you agree to carry. The impact your involvement creates.

The TRI framework provides a practical structure for doing this. Trigger.

Responsibility. Impact. When consultants define their service using these elements, conversations move away from résumés and toward real outcomes.

Independent consulting often operates through two legitimate models. Some engagements require specialist execution under operational pressure. Others require advisory judgment that restores clarity and momentum when organizations become stuck.

Many consultants also discover that technical expertise alone is not always enough to move work forward. Practical project management disciplines, such as clarifying priorities, coordinating work, and making progress visible, often become a valuable secondary capability.

Clarity about what you do filters work as much as it attracts work.

What Comes Next

Once your service is defined, the structure must support it.

Independence requires more than clarity of offering. It requires legal, financial, and administrative foundations that protect you from avoidable fragility.

Chapter 7 moves into the minimum viable structure required to operate professionally and safely.

Chapter 7
The Minimum Viable Structure for Independent Consulting

Independent consulting does not require complexity.
It requires sufficiency.

Many professionals hesitate because they assume the structure must be elaborate. Others rush forward and build nothing. Both approaches create unnecessary stress.

The goal is not optimization.
The goal is operational stability.

Minimum viable structure means having enough infrastructure to operate professionally, protect yourself reasonably, and reduce avoidable friction, without turning your practice into a bureaucracy.

A Professional Advisory Note

Independent consulting increases autonomy. It also increases responsibility.

Business formation, liability exposure, tax elections, and insurance requirements vary by jurisdiction and personal circumstance. What is appropriate for one consultant may be inappropriate for another.

The guidance in this chapter is experiential and educational. It is not legal, tax, or financial advice. Before forming an entity, signing binding agreements, or making tax elections, consult qualified legal counsel and a certified public accountant licensed in your jurisdiction.

Professional independence includes knowing when to seek professional advice.

Choose a Simple, Appropriate Legal Structure

Structure determines how liability is separated and how income is treated.

It does not determine whether you are a real consultant.

Most independent consultants operate under one of three models:

- Sole proprietorship
- LLC
- Corporation, including S Corp elections in the U.S.

Early on, simplicity usually outperforms sophistication. The objective is not to engineer the perfect setup. It is to create clean separation, administrative clarity, and a structure that your professionals can support without friction.

Practical differences you will feel day to day

Sole proprietorship often means:

- Fast start, minimal setup
- Little separation between you and the business from a liability perspective
- Clean enough for some early work, but limited protection if something goes wrong

LLC often means:

- Cleaner separation and professional presentation
- Straightforward banking separation
- Typically, easier to operate cleanly as you grow

Corporation or S Corp style structures often mean:

- More formal administration

- Payroll considerations
- Often pursued when income level and tax strategy justify added overhead

You do not have to decide this alone. But you do need to be ready to discuss it intelligently.

Questions to bring to your first CPA or attorney conversation

Bring these questions to get actionable guidance quickly:

- What liability risks exist in my type of consulting and what structure best separates them
- What income level typically justifies more structure and ongoing administration
- If I expect to subcontract later, what structure supports that cleanly
- What will I need to do monthly and quarterly under each option
- What does clean payroll and distribution look like if an S Corp election is on the table
- What business insurance will clients in my space typically require, and should that influence the structure
- What state and local registrations apply where I live and where I work

Local registration and business licensing

Depending on your jurisdiction, you may also need:

- A general business license
- A home occupation permit if operating from a residence
- Local tax registration
- Zoning compliance documentation

Other jurisdictions require none of these.

The important point is not to assume. Check with your city, your county, if applicable, and your state business registration site. Compliance is usually simple and inexpensive. It is part of operating professionally.

Separate Business and Personal Finances Immediately

Blurring financial lines creates confusion faster than almost anything else in independent practice.

When business and personal funds mix, it becomes harder to understand profitability, tax exposure, and true operating costs. Stress rises because visibility disappears.

Separation is simple but powerful:

- Dedicated business checking account
- Dedicated business credit card
- All revenue deposited into the business account
- Intentional transfers to yourself

This is not about accounting purity. It is about decision clarity.

Bookkeeping Creates Financial Calm

Independent consulting generates irregular income and deductible expenses. Without disciplined tracking, surprises accumulate.

Financial anxiety rarely comes from low revenue. It comes from uncertainty. And uncertainty is often a bookkeeping problem in disguise.

You need to know:

- What came in
- What went out
- What is owed in taxes
- What runway exists
- Which clients are paying on time and which are not

When visibility is unclear, decision making deteriorates. You may hesitate to accept well-aligned work because you are unsure of the runway. Or you may accept misaligned work just to relieve short term cash pressure. Both reactions are driven by uncertainty, not strategy.

For many consultants, hiring a part-time bookkeeper early is not a luxury. It is protection. It keeps your records clean, reduces tax surprises, and frees mental bandwidth for delivery.

Quarterly tax planning should not be reactive. A CPA can help you estimate allocations based on income variability and reduce avoidable mistakes.

Invoicing and Payment Discipline

Cash flow is emotional in independent consulting. Even strong engagements can feel unstable if billing cadence is inconsistent or poorly managed.

Define early:

- Billing frequency
- Payment terms
- Time tracking requirements
- Approval process
- Expense and travel reimbursement rules, including receipts and timelines

Invoice consistently. Do not delay billing because delivery feels more important.

When payment is late

Late payment will happen. Following up is normal and professional.

A simple cadence works:

- Follow up the day terms are met, polite and short
- Follow up again one week later, with the invoice attached
- If there is an intermediary, involve the recruiter or account manager early rather than letting it drift

- Keep language factual: invoice number, date, amount, and request for a clear payment date

The goal is not pressure. The goal is predictability.

A simple operating stack

You do not need a complex toolset, but you do need a clean baseline:

- Professional email with your own domain
- Secure document storage for your contracts, invoices, and administrative records (client materials should remain in approved client systems)
- An invoicing and bookkeeping system, even if simple
- A basic template set: invoice, statement of work recap email, status update email, and scope clarification email
- A single place to track receivables and follow-ups

Sufficiency beats sophistication.

Financial Runway Protects Judgment

Revenue volatility is normal in independent consulting. Engagements end early. Decision cycles slow. Hiring pauses appear. Projects get postponed. This is a structural reality, not personal failure.

What determines stress is not whether slow periods occur. It is whether you are prepared for variability before it arrives.

Runway is not about lifestyle comfort. It is about protecting decision quality.

Without a runway, you negotiate from urgency.

With runway, you negotiate from structure.

Consultants with modest reserves tend to:

- Decline misaligned work more confidently
- Resist rate compression during slow periods
- Avoid emotional pricing decisions
- Maintain a professional tone under pressure

Consultants without a runway often drift into:

- Panic driven discounting
- Overcommitment to unstable clients
- Exhaustion from stacking short engagements
- Acceptance of responsibility misaligned with compensation

Runway buys time. Time protects judgment.

A practical benchmark many independents use is measured in months of personal expenses, not months of revenue. Your number depends on obligations, risk tolerance, and how quickly your market typically converts opportunities into signed work.

Slow periods are inevitable. Financial panic is not.

Health Insurance and Benefits Reality

In employment, benefits are invisible until they disappear.

Health insurance is often the single largest structural cost increase when someone goes independent. It also changes how much runway you need, because premiums and out-of-pocket exposure do not pause during slow periods.

Do not treat this as a later detail. Research options before leaving employment. Common pathways include marketplace plans, transitional coverage during the switch, and coverage through a spouse or partner if available.

This is not a recommendation of any specific option. It is a reminder that benefits planning is part of readiness, not an afterthought.

Insurance: Quiet but Necessary

Employment absorbs risk invisibly. Independent consulting does not.

Many clients require proof of insurance before you can start. This is not theoretical. It can become a gating item during onboarding.

Common categories include:

Professional liability, also called errors and omissions
Covers claims that your work, advice, or deliverables caused financial harm.

General liability
Covers physical injury or property damage claims. Less common for pure remote IT work, but sometimes required by client policy.

Cyber liability
Covers certain data and security related incidents. This can matter when you access production systems, handle sensitive data, or are required to meet a client security standard.

Insurance is not paranoia. It is a professional overhead. Work with an insurance advisor familiar with consulting risk in your field and jurisdiction. The goal is appropriate coverage, not maximal coverage.

Contracts and Statements of Work

Earlier chapters covered scope, responsibility, and expectation management. Those principles become concrete in written agreements.

Verbal alignment is not sufficient protection. Ensure scope, rate, term, ownership language, and responsibility boundaries are documented clearly.

If the language is unfamiliar or broad, seek legal review before signing. Understanding your contract is part of your responsibility model.

Record Retention and Administrative Hygiene

Independent practice produces documents that matter later:

- Contracts and SOWs
- Invoices and proof of payment
- Tax documents
- Expense receipts
- Deliverables that may be referenced in disputes or audits

Create a simple retention habit. Keep a clean folder structure. Store signed agreements and invoices in a way that makes them easy to retrieve. The goal is not bureaucracy. The goal is to be able to answer questions without scrambling.

Retention requirements vary by jurisdiction, so ask your CPA what to keep and how long. Then follow that rule consistently.

Certification and Skills Maintenance

In employment, training budgets and certification tracking are often handled for you. In independence, they are yours.

Remaining relevant in your specialty requires a continual learning mindset. Systems evolve, tools change, and clients expect the consultant they bring in to already be current. Maintaining that readiness is part of the professional responsibility that comes with independence.

Some clients require specific certifications. Other situations simply require proof that your skills remain current. Without regular upkeep, credibility can slowly erode as technologies and practices move forward.

Plan modest time and budget each year for skill maintenance and certification renewal. Doing this intentionally prevents a common problem: being forced to schedule training or exam preparation while you are fully committed to client delivery.

During active engagements, your schedule is typically focused on project work, meetings, and deliverables. Trying to fit certification renewals or technical training into those periods often leads to rushed preparation or missed renewal windows.

Treat skills maintenance as part of the structure of your practice. A small amount of planned upkeep prevents avoidable opportunity loss and helps ensure you are ready when the right engagement appears.

Contingency Planning

In employment, illness or emergencies are buffered by paid leave, coworkers, and disability coverage. In independence, the buffer exists only if you create it.

Minimum viable planning:

- Know who you will notify if you cannot work suddenly
- Keep engagement status documented so someone can understand where things stand
- Consider whether short-term disability coverage is appropriate for your situation, and discuss it with a qualified advisor

You are not planning for a catastrophe. You are planning for continuity.

Keep Overhead Intentionally Low

Early independence often invites premature expansion:

- Office space
- Overbuilt software stacks
- Branding agencies
- Unnecessary subscriptions

Most of it is optional. A lean structure increases flexibility. Flexibility increases longevity.

Subcontracting, however, is different from overhead. Used thoughtfully, it can expand your capability without permanently increasing your cost structure.

Many independent consultants eventually reach a point where an engagement requires additional expertise and capacity, or a specific role the client expects to be filled. Bringing in a trusted subcontractor can allow you to accept opportunities that would otherwise be too large or too specialized to deliver alone. In many cases, it benefits everyone involved. The client receives the expertise they need, the subcontractor gains meaningful work, and you extend the scope and stability of the engagement. For many independents, this approach meaningfully increases revenue consistency and extends financial runway during active project periods.

At the same time, subcontracting does change the operating model. Once another consultant is delivering work under your agreement, you carry responsibility for coordination, payment timing, and delivery outcomes. This introduces additional considerations such as contractual structure, cash flow timing between client payments and subcontractor invoices, and ensuring that anyone working under your name is someone you trust professionally.

Used carefully, subcontracting is not a liability. It is one of the most practical ways an independent consultant can scale selectively while keeping fixed overhead low.

Chapter Summary

Minimum viable structure is not sophistication; it is stability.

Independent consulting requires a small set of structural foundations: clear legal separation, clean financial tracking, consistent invoicing, appropriate insurance, and basic administrative discipline.

These elements are not about bureaucracy. They exist to protect judgment.

When finances are visible, obligations are clear, and professional risk is managed, consultants make better decisions about clients, pricing, and opportunities.

Structure also supports sustainability. Maintaining relevant skills, planning for variability through financial runway, and selectively expanding through trusted subcontractors allow an independent practice to adapt without becoming fragile.

Structure does not generate revenue. Weak structure destroys it.

When the structure is clean, mental bandwidth returns to the work that actually matters: solving problems, delivering value, and building trust with clients.

What Comes Next

The next chapter moves from structural decisions to practical reality: what your work actually feels like day to day, across intense delivery, advisory judgment, and quieter maintenance phases.

That is the focus of Chapter 8 — A Day in the Life of an Independent Consultant.

Chapter 8
A Day in the Life of an Independent Consultant

Once your service is defined clearly, the question becomes practical: What does the work actually feel like?

Independent consulting does not have a typical day. What it has are patterns.

Different kinds of days appear depending on where you are in an engagement, what kind of responsibility you are carrying, and what pressure the client is under.

Many professionals imagine independent consulting as a steady stream of execution work. Others imagine constant strategy conversations.

The reality is uneven.

Some days are intense and reactive. Others are quiet and reflective. Some feel productive because output is visible. Others feel uncertain because the work happens internally before it becomes visible.

This chapter is not about productivity systems or personal routines.

It is about recognizing the kinds of days that make up independent work and understanding what each one is doing for you.

The Three Types of Days

Over time, most independent consultants notice something important. Not all productive days look the same.

Across industries and engagement types, most consulting days fall into three categories:

- **Delivery Mode** – execution and problem solving
- **Advisory Mode** – judgment and decision support
- **Positioning Mode** – sustaining the practice

The mix changes over time. Early independence tends to be delivery-heavy. As experience compounds, advisory and positioning days increase.

None of these days are better than the others.

Each serves a different purpose.

The mistake is expecting every day to feel the same.

Delivery Mode

Execution Under Pressure

This is the day most IT professionals recognize immediately.

You open your laptop, and there are fourteen emails. Production ran overnight, and something broke. Or the month-end close failed. Or a test cycle exposed configuration errors that cascade into other modules.

You feel the weight of velocity.

People discovered the problem before you did. They want answers. Not analysis. Answers.

On these days, you are not thinking about positioning or long-term strategy. You are solving problems.

You ask:

- What is actually broken
- What is noise
- What is reversible
- What cannot be touched

In structured project environments, the pressure feels different but no less real.

Before the 2020 COVID-19 pandemic, many independent consultants spent a large portion of their time traveling to client sites. Weekly flights and extended on-site engagements were common across the industry.

The pandemic forced organizations to adopt remote collaboration at a scale few had attempted before. Many companies discovered that a significant portion of consulting work could be performed effectively without constant travel.

As a result, the consulting environment shifted. Today many engagements operate primarily in remote or hybrid models, with occasional on-site visits when face-to-face collaboration provides clear value.

For many independent consultants, this shift changed more than logistics. It changed the rhythm of the work. A consulting day that once started in an airport lounge may now begin with a video call from a home office. Travel still plays a role in certain engagements, particularly during critical project phases or relationship-building moments, but it is no longer the default starting point for every assignment. For many professionals, the ability to deliver meaningful work without constant travel has expanded both flexibility and sustainability in the consulting lifestyle.

Remote delivery environments can also introduce situations that traditional office consulting never encountered.

The Reality of Remote Work

Remote consulting offers a level of flexibility that earlier generations of consultants rarely experienced. Work can be delivered from a home office, temporary locations, or even while spending time in other parts of the world.

That flexibility, however, comes with its own unpredictability.

During one period I was working remotely from Costa Rica while supporting a client engagement. I had rented a small beach house that served as both a temporary home and workspace.

One morning I had an online training session scheduled with a client team. About ten minutes before the session was scheduled to begin, the tropical birds outside became unusually loud. The house had open louvered windows designed for airflow rather than sound isolation, so every noise carried directly inside.

Then the situation escalated.

In the empty lot next to the house, a group suddenly began playing very loud mariachi music.

With only minutes before the training session started, I had to improvise. I moved my laptop into a small bedroom and began stacking mattresses from the other rooms against the walls and windows in an attempt to muffle the sound. By the time the session began, I had essentially created a makeshift recording booth.

The session went well and the client never noticed the chaos outside the room. But it was a memorable reminder that remote consulting environments require planning.

Since then, whenever I deliver remote training or workshops, I make sure a quiet backup location is available nearby, often a hotel or co-working space, in case the unexpected happens.

Flexibility is one of the great advantages of modern consulting, but professionalism still requires controlling the environment where the work happens.

Despite the change in environment, the nature of a specialist delivery day remains the same.

On a typical delivery day, you may be in the build phase of an ERP implementation, leading a design workshop for manufacturing planning. The whiteboard fills quickly. Requirements conflict. The business wants flexibility. The system enforces logic.

You are translating ambiguity into configuration.

You may spend the morning:

- Leading a functional workshop
- Reconciling requirements across departments
- Negotiating scope boundaries
- Clarifying test scripts

The afternoon might be:

- Reviewing defect logs
- Coaching users through UAT
- Coordinating with developers on impact

These days produce visible output. Documents. Configurations. Fixes. Status updates.

They also produce a specific kind of fatigue.

Adrenaline first.

Then compression.

Then the crash when the immediate issue stabilizes.

Clients are buying speed to competence. They want someone who has seen this before and does not panic.

The risk of too many delivery days is absorption. You begin carrying more than you priced. Ownership expands quietly because you are reliable.

In enterprise systems work, these are the days when production issues, configuration decisions, and operational pressure converge at the same time.

Early-career independents often measure their value by how exhausted they are at the end of these days.

Experienced independents measure value by how calmly they handled them.

Advisory Mode

Judgment Under Uncertainty

Advisory days look quiet from the outside and heavy from the inside.

You may spend three hours preparing for a thirty-minute meeting. You reread notes. You replay conversations. You examine where initiatives stalled. You map the decision tree in your head.

There is no ticket queue.

There is uncertainty.

You are not being paid to execute steps. You are being trusted to reduce ambiguity.

A typical advisory day may include:

- One or two focused conversations
- Long stretches of thinking
- Framing tradeoffs
- Drafting a short memo that took hours to clarify

The visible output might be three slides.

The invisible work is judgment.

What does it feel like?

Weight.

You walk into a meeting knowing your recommendation could shift a $2 million initiative.

You speak. You watch the room. You notice who leans forward and who looks away.

After the meeting, there is a period of decompression.

Sometimes relief. Sometimes second-guessing. Sometimes silence while leadership processes what you said.

Many new consultants misinterpret advisory days as underperformance because they do not look busy.

In reality, this is where responsibility concentrates.

Delivery days test skill. Advisory days test judgment.

The fatigue here is different. It is cognitive rather than reactive. You do not collapse at the end of the day. You feel mentally stretched.

Over time, pattern recognition makes these days less anxious. Early in independence, they can feel exposed.

Positioning Mode

Invisible but Necessary

Then there are days without urgency.

No client escalation. No high-stakes meeting.

Early in independence, these days can trigger doubt.

If no one is calling, am I relevant?

If I am not billing today, am I falling behind?

Experienced consultants understand something new; independents often do not:

Quiet days protect the practice.

A positioning or maintenance day may include:

- Reconnecting with a former client without asking for anything
- Reconnecting with colleagues
- Updating your service language to reflect recent patterns
- Writing a short reflection to clarify your thinking
- Reviewing insurance renewals
- Cleaning up invoicing records
- Studying a system update before a client asks about it
- Preparing a capability summary before you need it

These activities are not marketing stunts.

They are calibration.

One option during maintenance periods is writing. A short article, a technical note, or a brief reflection on a recent project can reinforce your professional visibility. It does not need to be long or polished to perfection. A few clear paragraphs shared on a professional platform can remind your network what you do and how you think about problems in your field. Over time, these small contributions accumulate. They help others associate your name with a specific area of expertise, which quietly strengthens future opportunities.

These days rarely produce immediate revenue. They produce future stability.

Too few of them and you drift into dependency. Too many of them early in your career and anxiety increases because the pipeline is thin.

By year five, these days feel strategic. By year one, they feel risky.

That difference is not structural. It is psychological.

When the Different Days Collide

Real independence rarely gives you one clean day type at a time.

You are in the middle of a production stabilization call and a recruiter calls with an opportunity you have been waiting for.

You scheduled a positioning day and a client escalation explodes your calendar. You are deep in advisory preparation and a technical defect drags you back into execution. This is normal.

The skill is not eliminating collision. It is managing it.

Experienced independents:

- Protect thinking time when stakes are high
- Do not answer every notification instantly
- Communicate clearly when focus is required elsewhere
- Schedule administrative work deliberately rather than squeezing it into exhaustion

The transition between day types is one of the hardest parts of independent consulting.

Switching from deep technical execution to strategic synthesis to self-directed practice maintenance requires mental gear changes.

No one manages that for you.

The Administrative Layer No One Talks About

Employment hides administrative weight. Independence exposes it.

On any given week you may need to:

- Send invoices
- Reconcile expenses
- Review contracts
- Respond to recruiter inquiries
- Renew insurance
- Track certifications
- Pay quarterly taxes
- Follow up with a recruiter

These tasks compete with client work.

Early in independence, many consultants push them to evenings or weekends. Then resentment builds because the workday never feels finished.

Experienced independents batch them. They treat administrative work as part of delivery, not a distraction from it.

Professionalism includes billing on time.

It also includes maintaining the structure that allows your practice to operate smoothly.

Administrative work is not exciting, but it is stabilizing.

Handled consistently, it prevents small obligations from becoming large distractions.

The Isolation Factor

No hallway conversations.

No shared lunch.

No team celebration when a go-live succeeds.

Independence can be quieter than expected.

Some thrive in that autonomy. Others underestimate the psychological shift. In a corporate environment, conversation happens naturally. Questions are asked in passing. Ideas are tested casually. Small signals from others help you gauge whether your thinking is on track.

Independence removes much of that background feedback.

For some consultants, the quiet becomes a productive space. For others, it can slowly feel isolating, especially during long engagements where most interaction happens through structured meetings rather than informal conversation.

This is where your professional circle matters. The peers, mentors, and former colleagues you speak with regularly.

Not for work but for calibration.

A short conversation with someone who understands your field can reset perspective faster than hours of solitary thinking.

Independence without conversation becomes echo chamber thinking. Structured peer contact protects judgment.

Early Career vs Established Independence

The structure of independent consulting stays surprisingly consistent over time. What changes is how you experience it.

The same kinds of days appear in year one as in year five. Delivery work, advisory conversations, and positioning activity are always present. What evolves is your comfort with them.

The same day feels different at different stages.

Year one:

- Delivery days feel intense because you are still calibrating boundaries
- Advisory days feel exposed
- Positioning days feel financially dangerous

Year five:

- Delivery days feel familiar
- Advisory days feel earned
- Positioning days feel strategic

Nothing about the structure changes.

Your tolerance for variability does.

Why This Mix Matters

Independent consulting is sustainable only when all three types of days are allowed to exist.

Too many delivery days lead to exhaustion. Too many advisory days without operational grounding, lead to advice that becomes too theoretical.

Too few positioning days create dependency and urgency. Too few delivery days erode operational credibility.

Recognizing which kind of day you are in, prevents you from misjudging its value.

A quiet day is not failure. An intense day is not proof of value. Each type serves a different function in a healthy independent practice.

Chapter Summary

Independent consulting does not have a typical day. It has patterns.

Most days fall into three categories: delivery under pressure, judgment under ambiguity, and maintenance that protects the future.

The mistake is not the mix.

The mistake is expecting every day to feel productive in the same way.

Delivery builds trust in the moment.

Advisory reduces uncertainty.

Maintenance protects sustainability.

Recognize the day you are in. Let it do its job.

What Comes Next

Once you understand the rhythm of consulting work, a sharper question appears.

What is this worth?

Pricing is not a number. It is the boundary that defines what responsibility you will absorb and what you will not.

Chapter 9 moves into pricing as a structural discipline rather than personal negotiation.

That is the work of Pricing Your Services.

Part V
Running the
Engagement Professionally

Pricing responsibility correctly, protecting scope, managing expectations, and closing work cleanly.

Chapter 9
Pricing Your Services

Pricing is not the first challenge independent consultants encounter. It is the first one they feel personally.

When you have spent years operating inside salary bands, internal equity models, and annual review cycles, pricing introduces a different kind of exposure. There is no institutional framework buffering the decision. No manager is calibrating the number. The responsibility sits entirely with you.

Your rate is not a statement of your worth. It is a boundary around your time, attention, and liability.

Market signals exist. Recruiters, colleagues, job postings, and other consultants provide a baseline. Most experienced professionals can identify a reasonable range quickly.

The real problem does not begin with the number.

It begins when the engagement asks for more responsibility than the number was designed to carry.

Recruiters often surface rate early, before you have context. The temptation is to answer quickly and sort it out later. Later is where misalignment accumulates.

A better approach sounds calm:

"I'm happy to discuss rates, but first I need to understand scope, expectations, and decision ownership. Otherwise, the number won't mean much."

That sentence is more useful than any negotiation tactic.

Price is not only the rate. It includes payment terms, availability expectations, travel expectations, termination language, expense treatment, and how adjustments happen when scope changes.

Occasionally, an opportunity will be offered on an "all-inclusive" basis, meaning travel costs are not reimbursed separately and are expected to be covered within your rate. This is not automatically unreasonable, but it changes the economics of the engagement. Flights, hotels, rental cars, and meals can consume a meaningful portion of revenue if they are not priced correctly. If an engagement requires travel under an all-inclusive structure, calculate the expected travel cost carefully and ensure the rate reflects that reality.

Travel also consumes time. Early-career consultants often account for airfare and hotels but forget that travel days themselves carry a cost. Airport time, delays, and late return flights can turn a four-day onsite engagement into a five-day commitment. If travel is required, make sure both the expenses and the time expectations are reflected in how the engagement is priced.

The Statement of Work Is the Pricing Anchor

Rates are discussed in conversation.

Responsibility is enforced in writing.

The Statement of Work governs what was agreed upon: scope, deliverables, decision ownership, availability expectations, and compensation. It is the document that translates pricing into operational reality.

Most pricing friction is not because an hourly number was "wrong." It is because the work being carried no longer matches the work being described.

A clear SOW protects both sides. It defines:

- what is included
- what is excluded

- who owns decisions and approvals
- what "availability" actually means
- how changes are handled

A rate that erodes trust, energy, or authority is not competitive. It is expensive in ways that do not show up on an invoice.

The missing skill: change orders in real life

Scope does not change on paper first. It changes in conversation. It changes in meetings. It changes in what people start expecting from you.

A change order does not have to be a formal document on day one. It can start as a clean checkpoint.

What it sounds like:

"I want to flag a shift. The work is moving from execution support into decision ownership. I can continue, but we should align the scope and pricing to match the role that's emerging. We have two options: narrow back to the original scope, or expand the scope and adjust terms."

That is not adversarial. It is maintenance.

When to raise it:

- When the client begins asking you to lead decisions, not just execute tasks
- When "quick questions" turn into recurring reliance
- When you are being held accountable for outcomes you do not control
- When availability expectations expand beyond what was agreed

Do it early. Drift is easier to correct at week two than at month three.

The Most Common Pricing Failure in IT Consulting

The most common pricing failure is not charging too little.
It is accepting advisory responsibility at execution rates.

This happens quietly and predictably.

A consultant is brought in for hands-on delivery, staff augmentation, support, or execution. The rate reflects that expectation. Early on, the work is bounded.

Then the shift begins.

The client asks:

- "What do you think we should do?"
- "Can you help us decide?"
- "You've seen this before, what's the right approach?"
- "Can you take the lead on this?"

None of these questions are unreasonable. They represent a change in responsibility. You are now being asked to frame problems, make tradeoffs, and absorb decision risk.

If it goes unaddressed:

- The consultant feels increasing pressure and fatigue
- The client becomes increasingly dependent

Neither side intended the imbalance. It emerges because the pricing model no longer matches the responsibility model.

What to do the moment you see it

Name the shift, then offer structure.

A direct version:

"I'm happy to step into that level of ownership. That's different from what we priced initially. Let's align on scope and terms so it stays clean for both of us."

If you are working through an intermediary, such as a recruiter, consulting firm, or staffing agency:

"I'm seeing the role shift from execution support into advisory ownership. I'm fine continuing, but we need a scope and rate adjustment to match the responsibility. Can you help facilitate that conversation?"

You are not "renegotiating because you feel like it." You are correcting an agreement that is no longer describing reality.

Your Rate is a Boundary

A common mistake is treating a rate as personal value. That creates defensiveness and unnecessary compromise.

Your rate is the boundary that defines:

- What responsibility you will carry
- How much uncertainty you will manage
- What availability you are committing
- What sustainability requires

If a rate requires you to overextend, overcommit, or silently absorb expanding responsibility, it is mispriced, regardless of how attractive it looks on paper.

The first time you say the number out loud

The discomfort is normal. You are not "bad at pricing." You are new at stating a boundary without an employer behind you.

Confidence here is not a personality trait. It is repetition.

Say your number plainly. Then stop talking.

Billing Models That Actually Matter

New consultants waste energy debating hourly vs daily vs fixed price. These distinctions matter less than people think.

What matters is whether the model matches:

- Predictability of scope
- Your control over sequencing
- Dependency and approval delays
- The amount of outcome risk you are carrying

Hourly or daily works well when scope is fluid, discovery continues, and priorities shift.

Fixed price works best when scope is stable, dependencies are known, and success criteria are explicit.

It also requires caution. Fixed price transfers delivery risk to the consultant. If scope expands, approvals slow, or external dependencies shift, the economics of the work can deteriorate quickly. Many experienced consultants use fixed price selectively and only when the boundaries of the work are unusually clear.

Retainers

Retainers fit advisory work when the value is not "hours logged." The value is access to judgment.

A retainer can mean:

- A monthly fee for defined availability and decision support
- A clear scope of issues you will cover
- Explicit boundaries for what triggers additional billing

Retainers fail when they are vague. They succeed when the agreement is explicit about access, response expectations, and what is out of scope.

The billing unit is not the risk.

Misalignment is.

Entry Pricing and the Precedent Trap

Many professionals worry about starting too high.

Entry pricing usually fails for the opposite reason: it is too low for the responsibility that predictably arrives.

A modest initial rate can be appropriate if responsibility is genuinely limited and learning is part of the value exchange.

But entry pricing has a hidden consequence:

The first number becomes the anchor.

If you price your first engagement with a client or recruiter low, that rate becomes the reference point for every future conversation. Raising it later is harder than starting correctly.

A useful self-check:

- If this engagement expands in scope or responsibility, as many do, would I still feel comfortable at this rate until the terms are formally adjusted?
- If the answer is no, the number is already misaligned.

Pushback Without Panic

Price pushback is not always rejection. Often it is a signal that something is unclear.

Before lowering a rate, clarify responsibility:

- "Which decisions do you expect me to own?"
- "How will success be measured?"
- "What happens when priorities shift?"

If the answers indicate execution only, the rate conversation becomes simpler.

If the answers indicate ownership, risk, and availability, the rate has to match that reality.

Not every engagement should close.

Recruiter pushback is different

A recruiter may push back because:

- The client has a budget ceiling they have not disclosed
- The recruiter is working within their own margin constraints
- They are pressure testing your confidence

Stay calm and ask for clarity:

"Is the client working within a specific budget range for this role?"

If the recruiter confirms a budget ceiling, you can decide whether the role and its constraints still fit.

If the answer remains vague, you have learned something important about the situation. You can hold your boundary or decide the opportunity is not the right fit.

The True Cost of Independence

A sustainable rate must cover what employment covered invisibly:

- Health insurance
- Retirement contributions
- Unpaid time off and sick days
- Training and certification maintenance
- Equipment and software
- Nonbillable hours and gaps between engagements

Do not compare your consulting rate to your salary.

Compare it to your fully loaded employment cost plus the reality that not every hour is billable.

When you have spent years operating inside salary bands, internal equity models, and annual review cycles, pricing introduces a different kind of exposure. There is no institutional framework buffering the decision. No manager is calibrating the number.

Independence also introduces costs that employment previously absorbed. Professional liability insurance, bookkeeping support, accounting and tax preparation, legal review, and other administrative services become part of operating your practice.

Your rate must support not only your time, but the infrastructure that allows you to work professionally and sustainably.

This is why a rate that looks high to an employee can be merely sustainable for an independent.

Rate Compression and Downturns

Markets soften. Recruiter calls slow. Clients push rates down.

When that happens, you have three clean options:

1. Hold rate and accept longer gaps
2. Reduce rate temporarily with explicit constraints
3. Accept lower rates only for narrowly scoped, low responsibility work

The trap is lowering your rate while keeping your responsibility wide. If you take a lower rate in a soft market, protect yourself with tighter scope, tighter availability, and shorter commitments.

Pricing as a Long-term Design Choice

Sustainable consulting is rarely built on heroic rates or constant negotiation. It is built on consistency.

Consistency in:

- How responsibility is priced
- How boundaries are enforced
- How adjustments are handled
- How often exceptions are made

Each exception teaches clients what to expect next time. Over time, your pricing behavior becomes part of your reputation.

When and how rates rise

Rate increases are simplest with new clients.

With existing clients or long-standing recruiters, raise rates by tying the change to reality:

- Expanded responsibility
- Increased demand and limited availability
- A new scope or phase of work
- A defined annual adjustment point

What it sounds like:

"My rate is now X for new engagements starting after [date]. For anything already in flight, we can keep the current rate through the current phase and align terms for the next phase."

Calm. Direct. Professional.

The consultants who last are not the cheapest or the most expensive. They are the clearest.

Chapter Summary

Pricing is not a statement of worth. It is a boundary around responsibility, uncertainty, availability, and sustainability.

The most common pricing failure in IT consulting is accepting advisory responsibility at execution rates. When you see the shift, name it early and realign scope and terms before drift becomes resentment.

Pricing holds when it is anchored to written scope, paired with clear adjustment language, and reinforced through consistent boundaries.

What Comes Next

Rates only stay clean when scope stays clean.

But scope cannot be written well until discovery makes reality visible. The next chapter focuses on the discipline that turns ambiguity into boundaries: moving from discovery into scope that reflects what is true, not what is hoped.

That is the focus of Chapter 10 — From Discovery to Scope.

Chapter 10
From Discovery to Scope

Discovery creates clarity. Scope turns clarity into commitment.

Most scope problems are not caused by bad intent. They are caused by premature certainty. Everyone wants to move forward. Assumptions fill gaps. Language becomes optimistic. Work begins on foundations that were never examined.

Discovery is not interrogation. It is alignment. It is the step that prevents you from committing to responsibility you do not control.

Scope is not paperwork. It is a working boundary the engagement can return to when pressure rises.

Earlier chapters covered how to read an agreement and protect yourself from obvious scope language traps. This chapter does something different. It focuses on two skills that determine whether scope stays clean:

1. How to run discovery that reveals what is true, not what is hoped.
2. How to maintain scope as reality changes.

What Discovery Is For

Discovery exists to answer two questions before you commit:

What is actually happening here?
What are you actually being asked to carry?

In execution-heavy work, discovery clarifies the operating environment: systems, integrations, constraints, timelines, and what is already decided.

In advisory work, discovery clarifies something else: why progress is not happening. The visible problem is often a symptom. The real constraint is usually decision-related, ownership-related, or expectation-related.

Good discovery names that without drama.

Two Discovery Tracks: Execution and Advisory

Discovery is not one-size-fits-all. It depends on what the client is really buying.

Track 1: Execution Discovery

Execution discovery answers: where do I plug in and how do I avoid being set up to fail?

Ask:

- Where does the work actually sit today?
- What is already decided and not open to change?
- What timelines exist and who owns them?
- What constraints are fixed? budget, tools, architecture, people
- Who owns prioritization?

Listen for a healthy environment sounds like:

- One person can name priorities without hesitation
- Access and decision paths are clear
- Constraints are stated as constraints, not vague warnings
- The problem statement is stable even if the solution is not

A concerning environment sounds like:

- Five people believe they own priority
- Nobody can explain how work enters your queue
- "Everything is urgent" language dominates
- Success is described as effort, not outcome
- Timelines exist but no one owns dependencies

What to do with the answer:

- If prioritization ownership is unclear, do not accept outcome promises. Scope to execution support within assigned priorities. Document that you do not own delivery success if you do not control sequencing.
- If constraints are fixed but unrealistic, do not argue them. Write them into assumptions. Let the scope reflect reality, not ambition.

Track 2: Advisory Discovery

Advisory discovery answers: why is this stalled and where does authority actually live?

Ask:

- Why have prior attempts failed?
- Where are decisions stalled?
- What assumptions are driving the current plan?
- Who carries real authority and who does not?
- What would have to be true for execution to become possible?

A healthy advisory environment sounds like:

- Leadership can name the decision they are avoiding
- Tradeoffs can be discussed without defensiveness
- Authority is not just titled, it is real
- Someone is willing to make calls and own the consequences

A concerning advisory environment sounds like:

- History is framed as "people issues" with no specifics
- Every failure is blamed on execution rather than decisions
- Authority is distributed, but accountability is not
- Nobody can state what success means in measurable terms
- Escalation paths exist on paper but not in practice

What to do with the answer:

- If the real constraint is governance, your scope cannot be "get the project back on track" unless the client is willing to change governance. Your scope becomes diagnosis, decision framing, and recommendation. Delivery stays separate unless authority and sponsorship are established.
- If decision authority is absent, your scope should include explicit limits: you can facilitate clarity, you cannot manufacture ownership.

The mistake is treating both tracks the same.

Execution discovery clarifies where to plug in.
Advisory discovery clarifies what must change before progress is possible.

What Good Discovery Produces

Good discovery produces three outcomes. If you do not have them, scope will drift no matter how carefully written.

- Shared understanding – you and the client can describe the problem the same way.
- Named assumptions and dependencies – constraints, unknowns, and critical dependencies are explicitly stated.
- Decision clarity - it is clear who decides what, and where escalation actually works.

When discovery fails, the engagement tends to follow a predictable pattern:

- Scope becomes optimistic instead of true
- You inherit dependencies you do not control
- Urgency begins substituting for decisions
- The client measures your performance against outcomes you never owned

Occasionally discovery is incomplete for a different reason. The operation itself may not yet exist.

New facilities are launched. New teams are still being hired. Processes are expected but not yet defined. In these environments, the consultant is asked to design systems before the organization has fully decided how it will operate.

When that happens, discovery cannot eliminate uncertainty. It can only make the assumptions visible.

The responsibility shifts from perfect understanding to disciplined documentation.

The following situation illustrates how that plays out in practice.

Occasionally, discovery begins without any defined scope at all.

The following situation illustrates how structure is created in real time, before the work is fully understood.

I received a call from a recruiter I had worked with several times before. He had placed me on prior engagements and knew my background. He said he had a client who needed help.

As always, I asked questions to understand the situation. What problem are they trying to solve? What are they trying to accomplish? What is the scope?

His response was simple. "They will tell you when you arrive."

That was all the information available.

Situations like this are not unusual in consulting. Not every engagement begins with a clearly defined scope. Sometimes the work starts with a conversation.

I agreed to meet with the client.

When I arrived at the facility, I was greeted by the IT Manager and brought into a conference room. It was one of the most well-designed conference rooms I had seen. Everything about the environment reflected a well-run organization.

A few minutes later, the CFO and Operations Manager joined us.

The CFO opened the conversation directly. "We need help."

I said, "Let's start from the beginning of your situation."

He explained, "We are building a new facility out of state. We need the ERP system set up for that location."

At that point, there was no defined scope. No documented plan. No detailed requirements. Just a clear objective and a significant number of unknowns.

I asked, "What do we know so far about the plan for this initiative?"

As we started the discussion, I stood up and asked, "May I use your whiteboard?"

"Of course," the CFO said. "It's all yours."

I drew a circle in the center and asked, "What are we calling this site?"

"Tennessee," they said.

I labeled the circle "Tennessee" and began building outward.

From there, I created five primary branches:

- People
- Processes
- Systems
- Data
- Project Planning

Each of these became its own working category.

Under People, I asked, "Who are you initially thinking will be on the project team for this initiative?"

Under Processes, I started with scope boundaries.

"What functional areas are in scope? Finance, manufacturing, order entry, procurement, warehousing?"

Once that was established, I followed with:

- "What processes do you expect to mirror from your current operation, and where do you anticipate differences?"

Under Systems, I asked:

- "What version of the ERP system are you on?"
- "What systems are you planning to integrate into the ERP environment, such as scanner guns or third-party quality systems?"
- "How many system users are anticipated?"
- "Do you have existing documentation from the initial ERP implementation at this site?"

Under Data, I asked:

- "What data will need to be created or converted for this new site?"
- "Who owns data preparation, validation, and migration?"

Under Project Planning, I asked about timing, sequencing, and dependencies.

The purpose was not to finalize answers. It was to make the unknowns visible and organize the conversation into something structured.

Within that first session, we moved from "we need help" to a high-level view of what the initiative involved.

It was not a complete scope. It was the first version of one.

That distinction matters.

This was a high-level scope that required a deeper dive into detailed requirements and formal scoping later. But it created alignment around the work, the categories involved, and the questions that needed to be answered next.

My role on that engagement evolved into a cross-functional, multi-role position: project manager, consultant, and implementer. The work expanded as the initiative progressed.

About a year later, I was brought back to support a system upgrade.

That is how many consulting engagements begin. Not with clarity, but with the ability to create it.

That kind of unstructured entry point is one challenge. A different one arises when discovery is complete, but the operation itself has not yet taken shape.

Working with Limited Information

Not every implementation begins with a mature operation.

Occasionally, a consultant is asked to design a system for a manufacturing environment that does not yet fully exist.

In 2004, I was brought in to help implement the manufacturing and inventory modules of a JD Edwards ERP system for a transportation equipment manufacturer launching a new plant. The expectation was that the ERP system would be ready when production began.

The challenge was that the manufacturing operation itself was still being defined.

The company had not yet hired most of the production staff. Processes were not documented. Shop floor practices had not been finalized. In practical terms, I had one operational contact to work with, the Plant Manager. Even he was working largely from expectations about how the operation would function once the plant was staffed.

Yet the system still had to be built.

My responsibility covered the manufacturing and inventory side of the ERP configuration. That included work order management, inventory management, material requirements planning, bills of material, routings, capacity planning, shop floor reporting, work center setup, manufacturing accounting, and product costing. Other consultants were responsible for purchasing, order entry, finance, and other functional areas.

In a typical implementation, these configurations are based on established processes. In this case, many of the decisions were based on assumptions about what the future process would look like.

Situations like this require a different kind of discipline. When the process is uncertain, the assumptions must be made visible.

Every configuration decision was documented carefully. The design documentation clearly identified the assumptions being made, the source of the information, and the fact that the configuration could require adjustment once the plant began operating with a full production team.

This documentation was not about protecting myself from the client. It was about protecting the project from confusion later.

We moved through the implementation methodically. Configurations were validated through proof of concept scenarios and unit testing. The Plant Manager reviewed the outcomes and signed off on each stage as we progressed. My portion of the implementation was completed in about three months.

At the time, the system reflected the best understanding available.

Months later, once the plant began hiring staff and real production processes started to emerge, questions surfaced. The new team wanted to revisit aspects of the work order management setup and certain routing structures.

That was expected.

Because the original assumptions had been clearly documented, the conversation was straightforward. I was able to provide the design documentation showing the assumptions used at the time and the testing that had been completed with management approval.

The system had been configured exactly as agreed based on the information available during the implementation.

In consulting, working with incomplete information is sometimes unavoidable. When that happens, the responsibility shifts from certainty to clarity.

When assumptions are documented, tested, and approved, the system can evolve as the real operation develops without confusion about how earlier decisions were made.

Turning Discovery into Scope

By this point in the book, you already know the principle: scope is a boundary around responsibility. This section is about mechanics.

A strong scope answers four questions in plain language:

- What is included?
- What is excluded?
- Who owns decisions?
- What signals completion?

Before discovery vs after discovery

Before discovery, the scope often sounds like: "Consultant will support system stabilization."

After discovery, scope should sound like what you actually learned:
"Consultant will assess instability within the MRP planning process, identify contributing factors, and provide remediation options ranked by impact and effort. Consultant will implement the selected option as directed by the client's IT manager. Responsibility for prioritization,

resource allocation, and final decisions remains with the client. This engagement excludes module redesign outside the MRP scope unless explicitly added."

The improvement is not wordsmithing. It is specificity created by discovery.

Scope can include a discovery phase

Sometimes discovery is not a pre-step. It is the first deliverable.

When the environment is complex, the real problem is unclear, or decisions are high stakes, propose a short discovery phase with its own output:

- What you learned
- What is true vs assumed
- Risks and dependencies
- Recommended scope options for the next phase

This prevents the worst scoping mistake: committing to delivery before you know what delivery requires.

Common Scope Traps and What to Say

Even when discovery is strong, scope erodes if it is treated as static while reality changes.

The Helpful Expansion Trap

You solve one problem well. The client adds another, assuming the work continues naturally.

What it looks like: "Since you fixed that, can you also take a look at this other area?"

What to say:
"Happy to look. That's a new thread beyond what we scoped. I can either take it on by trading off against current priorities, or we can add it as an explicit scope item."

You are not billing for kindness. You are keeping reality visible.

The Ambiguous Support Trap

Support quietly becomes ownership.

What it looks like:

"We just need support," then you are running decisions, sequencing, and accountability.

What to say:

"I can support this in two different ways. Execution support means I implement within the priorities you set. Ownership support means I lead prioritization and decisions. Which one are you expecting?"

Make the choice explicit while it is still small.

The Silent Dependency Trap

You become the decision hub because everyone defers.

What it looks like: People stop deciding because you are competent.

What to say:

"I'm noticing decisions are routing through me that require internal ownership. I can frame options and recommend, but the decision needs an internal owner. Who should that be?"

This trap is rarely malicious. It is gravitational.

Scope Is a Living Boundary

Scope does not end when the engagement starts.

If scope is only written once, it becomes ceremonial. If it is revisited lightly, it becomes protective.

When to run a scope check

A scope check is triggered by change, not by a calendar. Run one when:

- A new stakeholder enters
- Priorities shift materially
- You are asked to attend governance meetings you were not scoped for
- Availability expectations expand
- The client begins asking for decision ownership
- Success criteria change midstream

What a scope check looks like

Most scope checks are not a renegotiation. They are a two-minute alignment moment followed by a short written recap.

Conversation:
"This feels like a shift from what we originally agreed. Let's pause and clarify what you want me to own."

Follow-up recap (simple, not legalistic):

- What changed
- What stays the same
- What tradeoff you are making if you add the new item
- Whether pricing or timeline needs adjustment

Used early, this prevents resentment later.

Three Worked Examples

These are not project management stories. They are discovery-to-scope stories.

Example 1: Staff Augmentation Reality Check

Initial ask: "We need an extra set of hands for the ERP implementation."

Discovery reveals:

- Priorities change weekly based on whoever escalates loudest
- There is no single owner of prioritization
- Delivery dates exist but nobody owns dependencies

Scope after discovery:

- Execution support within priorities assigned by a named client owner
- Time-based delivery, no outcome guarantees tied to dates you do not control
- Explicit exclusion of "project recovery ownership" unless added later
- Weekly priority confirmation as an operating requirement

Why it stays clean: You scoped to the reality of ownership, not the ambition of timelines.

Example 2: Advisory Reset

Initial ask: "Our implementation is stalled. We need you to get it back on track."

Discovery reveals:

- Leadership is split on the target operating model
- Decisions are avoided, not made
- The project is not stalled from lack of effort, it is stalled from lack of authority

Scope after discovery:

- Diagnose decision constraints and map where authority actually lives

- Facilitate alignment sessions and produce a decision memo
- Provide recommended sequencing options with risks and dependencies
- Explicitly exclude delivery ownership until sponsorship is confirmed

Why it stays clean: You did not promise execution success when the real obstacle was governance.

Example 3: Hybrid Engagement

Initial ask: "We need hands-on support for stabilization."

Discovery reveals:

- The technical issue is real
- But the recurring instability is caused by cross-team ownership gaps
- The client is already starting to ask for direction, not just execution

Scope after discovery:

- Execution support for stabilization tasks
- An explicit checkpoint clause: if decision ownership shifts toward advisory, scope and pricing are revisited
- Defined triggers for that checkpoint: steering committee participation, prioritization ownership, cross-team decision facilitation
- Written recap after each checkpoint

Why it stays clean: You planned for the most common reality: execution work that becomes advisory by gravity.

Each example shares one trait: scope reflects reality, not aspiration.

Why Scope Protects Relationships

Consultants often avoid tightening the scope because they fear damaging trust.

In reality, unclear scope damages trust far more reliably than firm boundaries.

Clients relax when they know:

- What you own
- What they own
- What success looks like

Scope clarity reduces anxiety on both sides.

Chapter Summary

Discovery creates shared understanding. Scope turns that understanding into a boundary around responsibility.

Execution discovery clarifies the environment, constraints, and prioritization ownership. Advisory discovery clarifies decision authority, stalled constraints, and the assumptions driving the plan.

Strong scope is ownership language. It states what is included, what is excluded, who decides what, and what completion looks like. Scope stays healthy when it is maintained as a living boundary, not treated as a one-time document.

What Comes Next

Even good scope does not freeze reality.

Pressure changes priorities. Stakeholders rotate. Trust increases reliance. Expectations drift. The next chapter focuses on what keeps engagements healthy after the start: noticing drift early, naming it calmly, and resetting alignment before resentment builds.

That is the work of Chapter 11 — Managing Expectations.

Chapter 11
Managing Expectations

Expectation management is the quiet discipline that determines whether consulting engagements stay healthy over time.

Most consulting engagements do not fail dramatically. They drift.

Expectations are rarely broken in a single moment. They erode through silence, delay, and unspoken assumptions. The work continues. The discomfort grows.

Managing expectations is not about over-communication. It is about relevant communication.

Three questions keep alignment intact:

- What changed?
- Why does it matter?
- Is a decision required?

Anything that does not answer at least one of these is noise.

The goal is early reset, not late repair.

Expectations Are an Emotional Contract

Formal agreements define scope, rate, and duration.

Expectations define something more subtle: how people believe the engagement should feel.

That emotional contract includes assumptions about responsiveness, initiative, ownership, how problems get surfaced, and how disagreement gets handled. None of this is written in an SOW. All of it shapes whether the engagement feels successful.

Expectation drift rarely announces itself. It shows up as signals.

Three emotional signals worth treating as data

Frustration masked as urgency. This often looks like:

- Everything becomes "ASAP"
- Short messages replace complete context
- Meetings get tighter and more tense
- People stop explaining and start demanding
- Escalation becomes the default communication style

Appreciation paired with increasing reliance. This often looks like:

- "You're the only one who really gets this"
- You get added to more email threads "just in case"
- You are pulled into decisions outside your original lane
- Your name becomes the shortcut for alignment
- Questions shift from "can you help" to "can you own"

Silence where decisions should be. This often looks like:

- Approvals stop moving
- Steering meetings disappear
- Leaders stop showing up but still expect progress
- Priorities become implied instead of stated
- You keep being asked to execute without clarity on what matters

These are not personality issues. They are expectation signals.

The Illusion of Alignment

Many consultants believe expectations are set once, during discovery or week one. They are not.

Alignment decays over time, especially when:

- Pressure increases
- Leadership attention shifts
- Dependencies fail
- New stakeholders arrive
- The consultant performs well and becomes trusted

Ironically, strong performance often accelerates drift. You solve something cleanly, confidence rises, and the client expands what they ask of you. Each expansion feels reasonable. The cumulative shift is structural.

This is how consultants wake up six weeks into an engagement wondering how they became accountable for outcomes they never agreed to own.

Common Expectation Drift Patterns

Three patterns appear repeatedly in IT consulting. Each one has an early phase that feels harmless. That is the moment to act.

Pattern 1: The Support Expansion

What it looks like early:

- You are copied on issues that are not yours
- "Quick question" requests become daily
- You are invited into meetings as the subject matter safety net
- People start waiting for your opinion before deciding

The tipping point:

- Escalations route directly to you
- "Support" turns into "ownership" without a decision

- You are blamed for outcomes you do not control

A reset that works:

"I'm happy to keep supporting this, but I want to clarify the responsibility level. Are you asking for execution support under the current scope, or are you asking me to own the outcome? Those are different commitments."

The follow-up that prevents THE backslide. After the conversation, send a short recap:

"Based on today's discussion, my role is execution support on X and Y. Decision ownership remains with (name). If ownership shifts, we'll revisit scope and terms."

This is not legal posturing. It is memory.

Production Environment Boundaries

One boundary many experienced consultants establish early is avoiding direct changes in a client's production system.

Production is the live environment where the business operates. Even a small configuration adjustment can have consequences that are difficult to predict in complex enterprise systems. When something breaks, the question quickly becomes who touched the system last.

For that reason, many independent consultants limit their role to analysis, recommendations, testing in non-production environments, and implementation guidance while client personnel perform the final production change.

Inquiry access to production data is usually reasonable. Direct modification is a different level of responsibility.

A simple way to state the boundary is:

"I'm happy to review the issue, recommend the change, and help test it in a safe environment. For production updates, I recommend that someone on the internal team execute the change."

This is not about avoiding work. It is about protecting both the consultant and the client from unnecessary operational risk.

Pattern 2: Availability Creep

What it looks like early:

- Messages arrive earlier and later than agreed
- Response time expectations tighten without being stated
- "Just a quick thing" starts landing after hours
- "Urgent" becomes the default tag

The tipping point:

- You feel on-call without agreeing to be on-call
- The engagement consumes attention outside billable time
- Your calm tone becomes harder to maintain

A reset that works:
"I'm noticing requests are consistently landing outside our agreed availability window. I can support that, but it changes the engagement structure. Do you want to keep after-hours requests as true exceptions, or do you want to define an on-call expectation?"

Two options you can propose immediately:

- Keep the boundary: "After-hours is for critical incidents only."
- Price the boundary change: "If you want ongoing after-hours coverage, we should add an availability component to scope and rate."

Pattern 3: The Authority Gap

What it looks like early:

- You are asked to "drive" an outcome, but no one can approve decisions
- Stakeholders disagree and defer
- Leaders want progress without owning tradeoffs
- The project moves, but decisions do not

The tipping point:

- You become the workaround for governance failure
- You carry pressure without authority
- You get measured on outcomes that require leadership behavior

A reset that works:

"I can move this forward, but the current constraint is decision ownership. I can frame options and recommend a path, but someone internally needs to own the decision and its tradeoffs. Who is that owner?"

If the answer is vague, you now have discovery: the engagement is advisory, not execution, and needs to be scoped as such.

A Real Example

During one ERP engagement with a multinational agricultural products manufacturer, I was asked to conduct a discovery workshop related to the product costing module.

The organization needed to determine whether to implement standard costing or actual costing within the ERP system. Their existing costing model was complex, and leadership wanted to understand how each approach would affect financial visibility and operational control.

The workshop quickly expanded into a training and evaluation session. Finance managers and directors in the room wanted to see both approaches before committing to a direction.

I provided training on how the ERP system handled standard costing and actual costing. We then walked through demonstrations using their own product structures so they could see how each model behaved.

Even after the demonstrations, the group remained uncertain.

They requested additional detail, so I prepared an Excel model showing how each approach would calculate cost under several production scenarios. We reviewed the calculations together.

Still no decision.

As the discussion continued, it became clear that the hesitation was not technical. There was visible disagreement among the managers in the room, and no one seemed willing to commit to a direction that might later be challenged by someone else.

The problem was not information. The problem was authority.

I recommended that the project management office bring the company's Chief Financial Officer into the discussion.

When the CFO joined the next session, the decision was made quickly.

The technical analysis had never been the obstacle. The real decision maker had simply not been in the room.

Reset vs. Recover

When expectations drift, consultants have two modes: reset or recover.

A reset happens early. It is calm, factual, and preventative.

A recovery happens later. It is heavier, more emotional, and more costly.

A reset sounds like:

"I want to pause and make sure we're aligned. It feels like expectations have shifted slightly from what we originally agreed."

A recovery sounds like: "This is no longer what we agreed to, and it's becoming unsustainable."

Experienced consultants aim for resets, not because they are softer, but because they are cheaper.

When to reset

Reset when:

- The first pattern appears twice
- A new stakeholder changes direction
- Responsibility begins expanding through reliance
- Urgency starts replacing decisions

Reset early, while trust still exists and nobody feels accused.

Dialogue Examples

Example 1: When "Support" Becomes Ownership

Client:

"Can you just take this over? You understand it best."

Consultant:

"I can absolutely help here. I want to clarify whether this is still support under the existing scope, or whether you're asking me to own the outcome. Those are different commitments."

Example 2: Availability Creep

Client:

"Can you respond to these tonight? We need answers by morning."

Consultant:

"I can do that tonight. Before we normalize it, let's decide what we want our availability agreement to be. If after-hours support is becoming routine, we should define it so expectations stay clean."

Example 3: The Authority Gap

Client:

"Can you get alignment across the teams and make this happen?"

Consultant:

"I can lead the alignment process and bring options forward. For it to stick, we need a single decision owner. Who will make the call when teams disagree?"

Each response does the same three things:

- acknowledges the need
- names the shift
- invites a decision

That is the structure.

Expectation Management Without Sounding Difficult

Most consultants avoid these conversations because they fear sounding rigid.

The key is framing expectation management as protection for outcomes, not resistance to work.

Language that works:

- "So, I focus on the right things…"
- "To avoid surprises later…"
- "So, we don't lose momentum…"
- "To keep this sustainable and predictable…"

Clarity is easier to accept when it is framed as care.

Documentation is Expectation Management

You do not need long documents. You need small records that reduce confusion.

Three lightweight tools do most of the work:

1. After-meeting recaps. Two or three bullets:

   - Priorities confirmed
   - Decisions made
   - Blockers and who owns them
   - Next decision required and by when

2. Weekly status in plain language. Write a short note that includes:
   - What moved
   - What is stuck
   - What decisions are needed
   - What risk is growing if decisions do not happen

3. A "decision log" when stakes are high. One line per decision:
   - What was decided
   - Who decided
   - Date
   - Implications

This is not bureaucracy. It is alignment that survives memory.

Managing Expectations with Intermediaries

If you are placed through a recruiter or consulting firm, expectation management becomes triangular.

The client may be shifting expectations while the intermediary remains unaware. That can trap you.

Loop the intermediary in when:

- Scope is expanding materially
- The client wants more availability or ownership
- Payment or approval processes are slipping
- You anticipate a formal change order or extension

Keep it clean:

"I'm seeing the role shift from execution support toward decision ownership. It's manageable, but it changes scope and pricing. I wanted you aware before it becomes friction."

Do not use intermediaries as threats. Use them as structure.

Managing Your Own Expectations

Consultants bring their own expectations into engagements:

- How decisions should be made
- How quickly people should respond
- How organized the client "should" be
- How rational the environment "should" feel

If your internal expectations are unrealistic, you will radiate frustration even when the client has not violated anything explicit.

The discipline is simple:
Name what is true. Stop negotiating with what should be true.

That keeps your tone clean and your judgment usable.

The Consultant's Responsibility Is to Surface Reality

Expectation management is not about enforcing rules. It is about surfacing reality early enough to respond intelligently.

That includes naming:

- Conflicting priorities
- Unavailable decision-makers
- Unrealistic timelines
- Scope pressure
- Emotional fatigue

Consultants do not fix these alone but they must name them. When expectations remain implicit, pressure becomes personal.

When Expectations Cannot Be Repaired

Not every engagement can be stabilized.

Warning signs that recovery may be impossible:

- Leadership is misaligned and unwilling to resolve it
- Authority is permanently unclear
- Scope expands but terms cannot be discussed
- Urgency is constant and unmanaged
- Decisions are avoided indefinitely while execution is still demanded

Exiting professionally, without blame or drama, is a skill.

A clean professional exit sequence

1. Name reality once, calmly
2. "This engagement is operating under expectations that don't match the original agreement."

3. Offer options

    "We can reset scope, adjust terms, or reduce responsibility back to the original lane."

4. Set a decision deadline

    "If we can't align by (date), I recommend we plan a transition."

5. Transition deliberately
    - Document current state
    - Hand off open items
    - Close access cleanly
    - Preserve tone and relationships

This is not failure. It is professional judgment.

Chapter Summary

Most consulting engagements do not fail dramatically. They drift.

Expectations function as an emotional contract layered on top of formal scope. They expand through silence, success, and unspoken assumptions about responsiveness, ownership, and availability.

Managing expectations is the discipline of surfacing reality early using three questions: what changed, why it matters, and whether a decision is required. The goal is early resets instead of late recoveries. Some engagements cannot be repaired when authority remains unclear or scope expands without willingness to adjust terms, and exiting professionally becomes part of sustaining a practice.

What Comes Next

Expectation management protects the engagement. But consulting also has another constraint: cognitive load.

Notes accumulate. Communication expands. Drafting and synthesis consume time. The next chapter explores a modern form of leverage: using AI tools carefully to reduce friction around the work while keeping judgment, confidentiality, and accountability intact.

That is the focus of Chapter 12 — The Consultant's New Leverage: AI Tools.

Chapter 12
The Consultant's New Leverage: AI Tools

Independent consulting is fundamentally cognitive work.

It requires synthesis under pressure, structured thinking in ambiguity, and clear communication when stakes are high. The constraint has never been access to information. It has always been time, energy, and clarity.

Leverage in consulting has never meant doing less thinking. It has meant spending more of your thinking where it matters.

AI tools, used correctly, can reduce friction around the work so your attention stays on judgment, tradeoffs, and decisions.

One principle comes first. The work still belongs to you. Your name is still on the recommendation. AI can accelerate preparation and drafting. It cannot carry responsibility.

Where AI Actually Helps in Consulting Work

AI is most useful on work that is necessary, repeatable, and time-consuming, but not where your professional judgment creates the highest value. In practice, it helps most in five areas.

Synthesis

Consulting generates a large volume of raw material:

- Interview notes
- Meeting transcripts

- Emails and chat threads
- Status updates
- Conflicting stakeholder perspectives

Turning that material into usable insight takes time.

AI can help with a first-pass synthesis:

- Identifying recurring themes
- Highlighting contradictions
- Surfacing implied risks
- Proposing follow-up questions
- Drafting a clear problem statement for review

You still validate the patterns. But you arrive at the thinking work faster.

A concrete example: you complete five stakeholder interviews on why a project stalled. You have twelve pages of notes and three competing narratives. You ask AI to summarize themes, list contradictions, and propose questions that would resolve the disagreement. You do not treat the output as truth. You treat it as an organized starting point. What used to take half a day becomes a focused hour, and your remaining time goes into judgment, not sorting.

Translation

A core consulting skill is explaining technical reality to non-technical stakeholders without losing accuracy.

AI can help with translation:

- Converting technical findings into executive language
- Emphasizing impact, risk, and decisions rather than mechanics
- Adjusting tone for different audiences
- Tightening long explanations without stripping nuance

The consultant remains responsible for correctness and calibration. The tool reduces drafting friction.

Preparation

High-stakes conversations are common in independent consulting:

- Scope boundary discussions
- Reset conversations
- Executive updates
- Delivery risk disclosures
- Change discussions mid-engagement

AI can help you prepare by:

- Pressure-testing your framing
- Simulating objections from a skeptical stakeholder
- Generating concise talking points
- Refining tone so the message lands cleanly

This does not replace thinking. It strengthens it.

Reusability

Consultants repeat the same shapes of work:

- Assessment report structures
- Discovery question sets
- Workshop agendas
- Status formats
- Scope and SOW language patterns
- Closeout checklists and handoff notes

AI can help turn strong one-time work into reusable structures that compound over time. Quiet days become practice-building days.

Research and Context Gathering

Some of the highest leverage happens before the first client meeting.

When you enter an unfamiliar industry, business model, or environment, AI can accelerate background preparation:

- Summarizing an industry's vocabulary and operating rhythms
- Explaining common metrics and constraints in that domain
- Generating questions that show you understand the landscape
- Helping you build a first-pass "what to learn next" map

This is not a substitute for primary sources or direct client context. It is a way to arrive sharper, faster.

What Hasn't Changed

Clients do not hire independent consultants because they lack information. They hire them because they lack clarity.

They need someone who can:

- Interpret incomplete signals
- Reduce ambiguity without oversimplifying
- Frame tradeoffs honestly
- Communicate calmly under pressure
- Take responsibility for recommendations

AI does not absorb accountability when a decision turns out poorly. Judgment remains human. Responsibility remains yours.

AI does not change the consultant's role. It changes the cost of supporting that role.

AI as a Thinking Partner, Not an Answer Engine

The most effective consultants do not use AI to get answers. They use it to challenge thinking.

Useful prompts sound less like: "What should I recommend?"

And more like:

- "What assumptions am I making?"

- "What objections would a skeptical stakeholder raise?"
- "What could fail if this is implemented as written?"
- "What am I not seeing because I'm pattern-matching too fast?"
- "If I'm wrong, where would I most likely be wrong?"

This use strengthens judgment rather than bypassing it.

It also reduces overconfidence, one of the most expensive risks in consulting.

Where AI Falls Short

AI consistently struggles in the places your value is highest.

It does not know:

- What your client cannot change
- Which stakeholders are threatened
- How much political capital exists
- Which deadlines are existential
- Where compromise quietly breaks trust

It can list tradeoffs. It cannot choose them responsibly.

This is why AI tends to amplify experienced consultants more than inexperienced ones. It does not level the field. It magnifies capability.

Professional Guardrails Matter More Than Tools

Independent consultants must hold higher standards than casual users. Three guardrails matter.

Confidentiality

If you would not share it with a junior associate, do not share it with an AI system.

Do not upload:

- Client-identifying information
- Proprietary processes
- Sensitive configurations
- Anything governed by NDA
- Anything your contract restricts

Anonymize aggressively, or do not use AI on that material at all.

One practical reality: some clients now include AI usage restrictions in contracts or security policies. Treat this like any other compliance requirement. If the client prohibits it, you do not do it.

Verification

Treat all output as draft. Verify:

- Facts
- Implied assumptions
- Conclusions
- Technical accuracy
- Tone and certainty level

Confident errors damage credibility faster than slow clarity.

Ownership

Everything delivered to a client must be defensible as your work. Using AI does not reduce responsibility. It increases the need for discernment.

Enterprise Tools, Client Policies, and "Approved Usage"

The safest approach is to assume nothing.

Some clients have approved enterprise AI environments. Others prohibit AI usage entirely for engagement material. Many are inconsistent.

A clean operating habit:

- Ask what tools are approved in the client environment
- Check the SOW and onboarding/security policies for AI clauses
- If unclear, default to non-use for client-specific content
- Keep AI usage focused on structure, drafting, and non-sensitive material

You are protecting trust and compliance, not proving a point.

If a Client Asks Whether You Use AI

As tools become more visible, clients may ask. The best answer is calm, factual, and unremarkable.

A professional response:

"I use AI tools the same way I use Excel or PowerPoint, as productivity tools for drafting and organization. My analysis and recommendations are based on experience and validated against your environment. I do not upload confidential client information, and I follow your policies on tool usage."

You do not need to evangelize tools. You need to protect trust.

Common Mistakes Consultants Make With AI

Most failures are predictable:

- Treating first output as final
- Using AI to compensate for lack of expertise
- Passing through work you cannot explain
- Introducing false certainty through tone
- Using AI on restricted material
- Assuming AI saves time on judgment

AI saves time on scaffolding. Judgment still takes time.

A Note on Longevity

Tools will change. Models will improve. Interfaces will evolve. What remains stable is the professional standard:

- Clarity over speed
- Judgment over activity
- Responsibility over output

AI is leverage only when it serves those principles.

Chapter Summary

AI tools do not replace consulting. They reduce friction around it.

Clients hire independent consultants for judgment, synthesis, and accountability under ambiguity. AI cannot absorb responsibility when decisions go poorly. Judgment remains human and personal.

Used well, AI supports five high-value areas: synthesis, translation, preparation, reusability, and context gathering. Used poorly, it creates confidentiality risk and credibility damage. Guardrails matter more than tool choice: protect client information, verify outputs, respect client policy, and ensure everything delivered is defensible as your work.

What Comes Next

Tools create leverage, but they do not change the consulting cycle.

Engagements still end. When they do, how you close them determines what the client remembers and whether future work remains possible.

That is the work of Chapter 13 — Closing the Engagement.

Chapter 13
Closing the Engagement

Independent consulting is cyclical.

Engagements begin, stabilize, evolve, and end. Most do not end because someone failed. They end because something changed.

A project reaches completion. A funding cycle closes. A leadership priority shifts. An internal resource returns. A temporary gap is filled.

Endings are structural.

But for independent consultants, especially early in practice, endings can feel personal. There is a reflex to interpret closure as evaluation.

Did I do enough? Did something go wrong? Was I replaced?

Most of the time, none of that is true.

Professional consultants learn a different stance. Closure is not a verdict. It is a phase of the engagement. And like every other phase, it requires intention.

This chapter is about ending work deliberately so reputation strengthens, trust consolidates, and future opportunities remain possible.

Why Closure Matters More Than You Think

Consultants spend enormous energy on landing engagements, stabilizing expectations, delivering value, and managing scope and pressure. Very few spend the same intentional energy on how work ends.

That is a mistake.

Closure is where reputation consolidates. It is where trust is either reinforced or quietly eroded. And it is where future opportunities are most often seeded, sometimes years later.

Clients rarely remember every deliverable. They remember how the work ended.

This connects directly to the truth most consultants learn late. Trust is not stored as a list of tasks. It is stored as a memory. The end of an engagement is the moment that becomes easiest to remember.

If the ending feels clean, the client remembers competence and control. If the ending feels messy, they remember friction, even if the work was strong.

Most Engagement Endings Are Not Judgments

It is important to internalize this early.

An engagement ending does not automatically mean dissatisfaction, underperformance, loss of trust, or diminished value.

Common reasons engagements end include funding cycles closing, internal staff returning, priorities shifting, leadership changes, and scope completing earlier than expected. Sometimes the engagement ends because the work succeeded. Sometimes it ends because conditions changed.

If you interpret every ending as failure, you will overreact. You will cling too long, or disengage poorly, or quietly resent the client for something that was never personal.

Professional consultants treat endings as a phase of work, not a verdict.

The Consultant's Objective at the End

Your objective at closure is not to extend the engagement at all costs.

Your objective is a clean handoff, documented clarity, reduced dependency, and a client who feels supported, not abandoned.

Consultants who close well are more likely to be invited back. That is not paradoxical. It makes sense. Clean closure leaves the client confident. Confidence is what brings people back.

What Good Closure Actually Looks Like

Strong closure has four elements. These are not bureaucratic requirements. They are relationship protection.

1. Clear Deliverables

As an engagement nears completion, ambiguity often increases. People assume everyone knows what has been done and what remains.

They rarely do.

A good close includes a short written summary that answers four questions. What was delivered. What is complete. What remains open. What decisions were made and why.

This is not defensive documentation. It is professional clarity. A simple example, paraphrased from a typical stabilization engagement, might read like this.

Closing Summary MRP Stabilization Support

Purpose
Stabilize MRP planning execution and reduce planning exceptions created

by configuration drift, inconsistent master data, and unclear ownership of planning decisions.

Delivered

Reviewed current planning parameters at item branch and planning family level and identified the three settings driving the majority of noise.

Aligned on a single ownership model for planning priorities and exception review.

Created a weekly exception review cadence and a simple triage guide used by planning and customer service.

Implemented two configuration changes in the planning module and validated results over two MRP cycles.

Documented the decision rationale for each change and what to monitor.

Open Items and Known Risks

Part number group B still carries inconsistent lead times due to supplier variability. This will continue to produce expedited signals unless lead times are maintained weekly.

Forecast consumption rules remain inconsistent across two branches. This was observed but not changed in this engagement.

Training for two new planners is not complete. A short runbook is provided, but confidence will improve with one additional guided cycle.

Deferred Work

Full forecast consumption redesign was discussed and intentionally deferred because it requires cross-functional approval and data cleanup that is not currently staffed. If pursued, it should begin as a separate assessment phase.

Next Step Options

Option A: maintain current cadence for four weeks and reassess stability.

Option B: perform a focused assessment on forecast consumption and branch alignment.

That is enough. Specific, calm, non-dramatic. It creates a shared record that protects both sides.

2. Knowledge Transfer Without Martyrdom

Independent consultants sometimes fall into a trap at the end. They try to transfer everything.

That is not realistic. It is also not required.

Your responsibility is to transfer what the client must have to own the next phase confidently.

Decisions. Rationale. Critical dependencies. Known failure points. How to maintain what exists. Where the documentation lives. How to detect drift early.

You are not required to recreate your entire mental model. You are not required to document every edge case. You are not required to train until no questions remain. You are not required to stay indefinitely just in case.

Here is what effective knowledge transfer often looks like in an IT consulting engagement when there is one week left.

Early week
You deliver a closing summary draft and ask the client owner to review it. This forces alignment on what is complete and what is not.

Mid week
You hold one structured walkthrough with the person taking over. The goal is not to impress them with depth. The goal is to transfer operating confidence. You walk through the decision rationale, the top failure points, and the monitoring cadence.

Late week
You provide a short runbook or operating notes and confirm escalation ownership. You do not promise availability beyond what is agreed. You simply ensure the baton has been passed.

This is supportive without creating an ongoing obligation. It respects the client's ownership while protecting your time and your practice.

There is one moment you will see repeatedly. The client says, "Can you stay one more week to make sure it is smooth?"

Sometimes the answer is yes. Sometimes it should be no. The professional response is to treat the request as a decision, not as guilt.

A calm answer sounds like this.

"I can support one additional week if you want that added stability. If we do that, let's define what success looks like for that week and confirm the extension terms, so it stays clean."

If you cannot or do not want to extend, you can still be generous without becoming indefinite.

I want the handoff to go well. We can do a final walkthrough and leave you with a clean runbook. After that, ownership sits with your team. If you need future support later, we can discuss a new scope.

3. A Clean Operational Handoff

Clients should know who owns what after you leave. They should know where documentation lives. They should know how to escalate known issues. They should know what assumptions still exist.

Ambiguous ownership after departure creates unnecessary risk and often resentment.

This is where many consultants accidentally burn trust. Not because they did poor work, but because they left the client anxious.

A simple handoff is often enough.

Owner after exit

Who owns the process. Who owns the system changes. Who owns the approvals. Who owns the monitoring cadence.

Artifacts

Where the final documents live, in one place, with names that make sense.

Escalation

If issue X happens, who decides what? If decision Y is required, where does it go?

4. A Professional Closing Conversation

Even when an ending is expected, a closing conversation matters. It does not need to be emotional or ceremonial. It needs to be clear.

A good closing conversation confirms three things. What we delivered. What remains open. Who owns the next phase.

A professional close can sound like this.

"As we approach the end of this engagement, I want to confirm what we delivered, what remains open, and make sure you feel comfortable owning the next phase. If you want a short transition window, we can define it cleanly."

That conversation reinforces control and competence on both sides.

It also gives you a moment to leave the relationship in a clean emotional state. The work ends, but the memory remains.

A Simple Closure Deliverables Checklist

You do not need a complex process. A simple structure works.

Most closures benefit from:

- A final summary document, often three to five pages
- Updated diagrams or artifacts that someone will actually use
- A decision log or rationale summary, even if short
- A list of risks to monitor
- Recommendations for next steps, optional and non-prescriptive

- A handoff note that names ownership after you leave

The tone matters. This is not a sales pitch. It is a professional wrap up.

What Undermines Closure

Poor closure usually comes from one of three patterns.

Drifting to the end

This is the most common. Nobody names the ending. Meetings get less frequent. Your calendar thins. Requests arrive slower, then oddly urgent. Ownership becomes unclear. You are still billing, but the work starts to feel like motion without direction.

Then the recruiter mentions casually that the client is winding down. You realize the engagement ended two weeks ago without anyone saying so.

If you have been through this, you recognize the feeling. It is not dramatic. It is awkward. And it creates a memory of fuzziness at the end, even if the middle was excellent.

Overstaying

Sometimes the consultant lingers without clear value, hoping to remain relevant. The work becomes small tasks, low leverage fixes, meetings that do not need you.

This is rarely good for anyone. The client begins to see you as overhead. You begin to feel unnecessary. That combination produces quiet resentment.

A clean end is stronger than a slow fade.

Abrupt exit

Sometimes the engagement ends suddenly and there is little documentation or transition. The client feels abandoned. The consultant feels defensive. Trust takes the hit.

Even when the ending is not your choice, you still control the tone and professionalism of the exit.

When the Ending Is Sudden

Not all endings are planned.

Sometimes a recruiter calls and says the client is freezing spend. Leadership changed direction. The project is paused indefinitely. Your access ends Friday.

This moment can hit hard, especially early in independence. You had three more months planned in your head. Your pipeline is empty. Your financial cushion suddenly becomes real.

Professional composure in that moment is not fake calm. It is discipline.

A good response has two layers. External professionalism and internal management.

Externally, stay calm and move immediately to closure questions.

What is the final day of access? Who is the client owner for the transition? What documentation would be most useful to them. Is there an approved short closure window for handoff? When will the final invoice be processed?

Then offer a tight closure plan.

"I understand. I can support a focused transition. I'll provide a closing summary, confirm ownership for open items, and do a final walkthrough with your designated owner if we can schedule it before access ends."

Internally, do not let panic write your next message. Sudden endings are one of the reasons you built runway and structure earlier in the book. This is where that discipline pays off.

Do not take sudden endings personally. How you respond matters more than why it happened.

As an independent consultant, project endings are inevitable. They happen in many ways, and how you respond defines your professionalism.

Final Invoice and Administrative Closure

Ending cleanly includes money, documents, and timing.

Send the final invoice promptly, ideally within 24 to 48 hours of the final day or final deliverable, depending on your billing cadence. If closure activities were part of the engagement, bill them. If you are offering a short closure window beyond the original end, treat it as scoped time, not as a favor that disappears on the invoice.

Confirm any reimbursable expenses and submit them in the same window. Loose ends in billing create friction that has nothing to do with your work quality and everything to do with memory.

If payment delays occur, handle it professionally and early. Courtesy follow up is normal. Silence signals weakness, not politeness.

Asking for a Reference or Testimonial

The closing conversation is the natural time to request future reference permission. Many consultants avoid this because it feels transactional. It does not have to.

The key is to ask it as a simple continuation of trust, not as seeking praise.

If you feel the work went well, I would appreciate being able to use you as a reference if a future client asks. Would that be okay. If so, who is the best person for that.

If a written testimonial fits the relationship, keep it light.

If you would be comfortable writing two or three sentences about what the engagement improved, that helps me a lot. If not, no problem at all.

Do not force it. But do not skip it out of discomfort. Done calmly, this is normal professional practice.

When the Client Asks You to Recommend Your Replacement

This happens often. It is a compliment and a risk.

If you recommend someone from your network, be clear about what you are and are not doing.

I can recommend a few people I trust. I'm not managing them. You'll still want to evaluate fit and confirm your own expectations.

If the situation shifts into subcontracting or placement, treat it as a formal decision, not as a casual favor. That belongs to your structure and agreements, not to goodwill alone.

The Personal Debrief

After closure, do not just move on. Harvest the data.

A short personal debrief, even fifteen minutes, compounds over time.

What went well? Where did the scope drift? Where did boundaries hold? Where did they break? What language worked? What language caused friction? What would you do differently next time.

Each closed engagement is a feedback loop that improves your service definition, your pricing clarity, and your expectation management.

That is how a practice gets better without drama.

Leaving the Door Open Professionally

Good closure does not chase future work. It makes future work possible.

Simple language works.

If conditions change and support is needed again, feel free to reach out. No pressure. No pitch. Just professionalism.

Clients remember restraint.

A year after completing an ERP project, the Director of IT at the end client contacted me directly. He asked if I would be interested in leading a system upgrade initiative.

I told him I was interested, but there was a constraint.

I had been placed on the original project through a consulting firm, and my agreement with them included a two-year non-compete. If they wanted to move forward, the conversation needed to go through that firm.

It would have been easy to bypass that step. The relationship was already established and the work was there.

Instead, the consulting firm reached out to me shortly after and placed me on the engagement.

The opportunity did not disappear; it followed the structure that made it possible.

Chapter Summary

Engagements end for structural reasons, not necessarily because something went wrong.

Professional closure is a phase of the work. It consolidates reputation, reduces dependency, and leaves the client feeling supported rather than abandoned. Strong closure includes clear deliverables, a realistic knowledge transfer, defined post engagement ownership, and a calm closing conversation that confirms what is complete and what remains open.

Poor closure usually comes from drifting to the end, overstaying without clear value, or exiting abruptly without transition. Sudden endings require composure and a short, focused closure window when possible. Clean closure also includes administrative discipline, final invoicing, and closing the loop on references when appropriate.

Consultants who close well are more likely to be invited back because they leave confidence behind.

What Comes Next

After closure comes a quieter phase that most professionals are not trained for.

The calendar opens. The inbox quiets. Silence invites urgency and distorted narratives. The next chapter focuses on managing the gap between engagements without rate panic, desperation signaling, or misaligned acceptance.

That is the work of Chapter 14 Managing the Gap.

Part VI
Sustainability and Longevity

Managing gaps between engagements and designing a consulting practice that lasts.

Chapter 14 — Managing the Gap

Chapter 15 — Building a Sustainable Practice

Chapter 14
Managing the Gap

Independent consulting does not reward constant motion. It rewards durability. And durability is tested in the gap.

The first time you experience a real gap, it can feel unsettling. Not because something is necessarily wrong, but because most professionals have spent their entire careers inside systems designed to hide volatility.

Between engagements, there is a phase most professionals are not trained for. No daily status calls. No urgent escalations. No visible deliverables. No immediate validation.

Just space.

Early in independence, that space feels dangerous.

The calendar opens. The inbox quiets. Recruiters who were active last month go silent. You check your email more often than usual. You refresh LinkedIn without admitting you are doing it. You replay the last engagement in your mind, looking for signals you might have missed.

This reaction is common and it is also misleading.

Most consulting engagements do not end because someone failed. They end because something structural shifted. A project concluded. A budget cycle closed. A staffing gap was filled. A corporate initiative lost priority. Leadership changed direction.

Employment hides volatility. Organizations absorb it.

Independence makes volatility visible. That visibility can feel like instability.

It is not. It is information.

A gap is not a verdict on your competence. It is part of the consulting cycle.

Engagement. Intensity. Closure. Gap. Re-entry.

That rhythm repeats across years.

The consultants who struggle most are not those who lack skill. They are those who misinterpret the gap. They treat it as scarcity, rejection, or urgency, and then make reactive decisions that erode the structure they worked hard to build.

The consultants who last understand something different.

The gap is not dead space. It is design space.

What the Gap Actually Feels Like Week by Week

The gap has stages. The danger is not any single emotion. The danger is what you do in response to it.

Week one: decompression and after echo

The first days can feel like relief. The engagement ended. The pressure released. You catch up on sleep. You take a breath.

Then the after echo arrives.

Your mind keeps running the last engagement anyway. You remember the escalation call. The tense meeting. The moment you solved something that mattered. The client saying thank you. Or not saying it.

In week one, the gap often feels like a doorway. You are not in the old work anymore, but you are not in the next work yet.

The skill here is simple.

Do not fill the silence too fast.

Week two: the itch

Week two is where many consultants start to itch. The relief wears off. The days start to look similar. You check for messages too often. The phone stays quiet.

Your brain wants to create a reason.

Was I replaced? Did I underperform? Is demand shrinking? Should I lower my rate? Should I pivot?

In week two, the gap starts writing stories. Your job is not to stop them. Your job is to recognize that they are assumptions, not signals. Silence is not proof—it is the absence of a signal.

Week three: interpretation begins

By week three, the gap starts becoming interpretive. You are no longer just noticing the silence. You are assigning meaning to it.

This is often where a consultant starts reviewing past conversations with too much intensity. A recruiter who said "I'll keep you in mind" now sounds dismissive in memory. A client who ended an engagement cleanly now feels like someone who may have been disappointed. Neutral signals start getting read as negative signals because the mind prefers a painful explanation over no explanation.

Week three is dangerous because nothing dramatic has happened, yet urgency begins consolidating.

The right move here is not more emotional analysis. It is a simple structure. Keep normal routines. Keep perspective. Reach out to the small group of people who actually matter. Resist the urge to make broad changes in response to incomplete information.

Week four: math becomes louder

By week four, the emotional tone changes. Now the gap touches money. Not because you are broke. Because your mind starts running the model.

How long can this go. What does my runway really cover. How many weeks until I need something to land.

This is where consultants either become steadier or become reactive.

The steady consultant uses week four to tighten structure. The reactive consultant uses week four to chase relief.

Week four is often where the gap stops feeling psychological and starts feeling operational. That is useful. It shifts the question from "What does this silence mean about me?" to "What does my model need from me right now?"

That is a healthier question.

Week eight: the character test

By week eight, if nothing has landed, the gap becomes a character test. This is where you can do everything right and still wait.

You can reach out calmly. Stay visible. Strengthen your assets. Keep relationships warm. Protect your pricing coherence. Keep your energy up. And still wait.

This stage is where many people make their most expensive decisions, not because they are careless, but because prolonged silence makes urgency feel rational.

It is not.

Week eight is where the tempting mistakes begin to look responsible. Lowering your rate feels practical. Accepting a vague role feels better than waiting. Broadening your positioning too far feels adaptive. Flooding your network with availability messages feels like action.

In reality, this is often the stage where poor decisions are made for emotional reasons and then explained later as strategy.

Doing it right at week eight usually looks less dramatic. You review runway honestly. You reduce unnecessary burn if needed. You stay connected to the few people closest to real demand. You continue refining how you describe your work. You protect your rate unless the change is intentional and tied to a real strategic reason. And you refuse to let silence talk you into misaligned work you already know is wrong.

If you can remain composed here, you have crossed a line. You are no longer practicing independence emotionally. You are living it.

The goal of independent consulting is not to eliminate uncertainty. It is to become steady inside it.

Gaps are Structural, not Personal

Every independent consultant will experience slow periods.

Even in strong markets. Even with a strong reputation. Even after a successful engagement.

Contracts end. Decision cycles extend. Internal resources return. Entire sectors contract simultaneously. Procurement slows. Projects pause while leadership reshuffles. Budget owners wait until next quarter to commit.

Most gaps are structural. Very few are personal.

When silence is interpreted as judgment, urgency follows. And urgency distorts decision making.

The mature move is restraint.

Restraint does not mean passivity. It means you act without panic. You make moves that protect your positioning rather than moves that soothe your nerves for a day and cost you for a year.

The Emotional Distortion of Silence

An open calendar invites stories.

Was I replaced? Did I underperform? Is demand shrinking? Should I lower my rate? Should I pivot immediately?

Silence creates narrative. Narrative creates urgency. Urgency creates reactive decisions.

That is the emotional distortion of a gap. The silence itself is rarely the real problem. The problem is the meaning you assign to it before you have enough evidence.

Experienced consultants eventually learn to treat silence as incomplete information rather than personal judgment. Once you accept that gaps happen in every practice, even strong ones, the silence loses some of its emotional authority.

The Two Failure Modes During a Gap

There are two predictable reactions. Both feel reasonable in the moment. Both create long-term damage.

Failure mode one rate compression

Rate compression rarely happens as a dramatic decision. It happens as a small concession that becomes an anchor.

A recruiter calls with something close but not quite. Lower rate. Shorter term. Unclear scope. You hesitate.

They say the market shifted. They say budgets are tight. They say the client has options.

You agree to a number that is fifteen percent below your standard because the alternative is more silence.

You tell yourself it is temporary.

Then a second recruiter asks your rate. You give the new number because now it is what you accepted last time.

Within two engagements, you have repositioned yourself downward. You did not intend to. You did not announce it. The market simply updated its understanding of you.

Climbing back takes longer than falling.

Temporary anxiety becomes long-term positioning damage.

A steady consultant can discount intentionally for a strategic reason. A new sector entry. A narrow scope with low responsibility. A short bridge engagement with clean boundaries. But that is a decision made with clarity.

Discounting as emotional relief is different. It is a nervous system decision disguised as strategy.

Failure mode two misaligned acceptance

This one is more painful because you usually know it is wrong when you say yes.

The scope is vague. Authority is unclear. The client wants outcomes but will not own decisions. The travel is heavier than you want. The role is responsibility heavy at execution pricing.

You feel the misalignment. Then you accept anyway because silence feels worse.

This is the trap.

Misaligned work does not just cost you energy. It costs you options.

The first week confirms your instinct. Meetings multiply. Decisions stall. You become the default owner without authority. You start working nights to protect the client from their own structure.

Three months later, you are tired, less visible to aligned opportunities, and less able to say no when the next misaligned call arrives.

Misaligned acceptance is not just a work problem. It is a rhythm problem. It turns the gap into panic and then turns the engagement into recovery debt.

A brief real-world pattern

Imagine a consultant at week six of a gap. A recruiter calls with a role that is lower rate, travel-heavy, and vaguely described as "helping drive the project." The consultant knows what that usually means. Ownership without authority. More availability than stated. Likely pressure with little structure.

Saying yes would relieve the discomfort of the gap immediately.

Saying no would preserve the ability to wait for something cleaner.

This is the kind of decision that defines whether a practice stays coherent. The gap does not damage the practice. Panic does.

What a Gap is Actually For

A gap is not downtime. It is maintenance.

When used well, gap periods create leverage. Not theoretical leverage. Real leverage that shows up later as better fit, cleaner scope, stronger rates, and less dependency.

There are five productive uses of a gap. You do not need to do all five. Pick one or two. Do them calmly.

Relationship maintenance without desperation

Your goal is not to tell the world you need work. Your goal is to remind the right people that you exist and what you do.

A calm note to a trusted recruiter can be simple.

I wrapped an engagement and will have availability starting next month. If you see needs aligned with manufacturing planning and operations support, I'm open to a conversation.

A calm note to a former client can be even simpler.

Hope you're doing well. I just finished an engagement and had you on my mind. If anything comes up where you want a second set of eyes, feel free to reach out.

The difference between calm outreach and scarcity signaling is tone and targeting. Calm outreach goes to a small list. Scarcity signaling goes to everyone.

Market sensing

During a gap, you have the rare advantage of observing the market without being buried in delivery.

Talk to two or three recruiters you trust and ask the same questions.

What roles are actually closing right now? What rates are holding? What is slowing approvals? Which industries are still spending?

You are not asking for reassurance. You are collecting signal.

Market sensing is useful because it helps you distinguish between a personal story and a market reality. If three good recruiters tell you approvals are dragging across the board, you have context. If one tells you your niche is quiet but adjacent demand is holding, you have information you can act on without abandoning your identity.

Service language refinement

The gap is the best time to update how you describe your service because you can do it without pressure.

Use your most recent engagement as the raw material.

What problem did you actually solve? What did the client value most? What did they rely on you for. Where did scope drift? What boundary mattered most?

Then tighten your service language so it reflects reality, not aspiration.

This might mean turning a vague statement like "ERP consulting support" into something more specific and credible. It might mean emphasizing planning stabilization, cross functional manufacturing alignment, or execution support inside a defined lane. The point is not to sound bigger. It is to sound truer.

Asset building

The best independents quietly build reusable assets that make future work cleaner.

A discovery question set you actually use. A status update format clients read. A closing summary template. A scope clause library. A short capability summary that fits in an email.

These are not busywork. They are compounding.

Asset building matters because it reduces friction later. A strong discovery checklist improves every new conversation. A clean scope clause protects future engagements. A simple recap format saves time every week once delivery starts. These tools do not look dramatic while you are building them. Their value appears later, when work is active and you no longer have to invent structure under pressure.

If you want to know what to do on a Monday during a gap, this is one answer: improve one reusable thing that your future self will use more than once.

Skill investment

Not broad learning. Targeted learning.

Pick one skill that would have helped in the last engagement. Deepen it. Then stop.

The gap is not a time to become a new person. It is a time to sharpen the person you already are.

That may mean learning one reporting capability you kept needing. Strengthening one domain in which you were weak. Deepening your understanding of a process, tool, or decision pattern that kept showing up in real work.

The mistake is treating the gap like a reinvention project. Most consultants do not need reinvention between engagements. They need sharper edges.

These days may not produce revenue. They produce leverage.

Strong consultants treat gaps as recalibration, not crisis.

A Gap Is Also Recovery

Not every gap needs to be optimized.

Some need to be absorbed.

Independent consulting compresses energy. Delivery phases are intense. Advisory work carries cognitive load that accumulates quietly. Even when engagements go well, they draw heavily on attention, judgment, and emotional steadiness.

When an engagement ends, that tension does not disappear immediately.

A gap can be used productively. It can also be used to reset.

That is not avoidance. It is maintenance.

For some consultants, reset means a change of environment. Working temporarily from somewhere quieter. Spending time in a different climate. Stepping away from daily noise.

It may be time to write. To reflect. To think clearly without interruption. It may be the right moment to deepen a skillset without client pressure.

And sometimes, the most responsible use of a gap is personal.

Taking your family on a needed vacation. Being present without checking email constantly. Letting your nervous system settle. Sleeping normally again. Exercising without squeezing it between calls. Allowing energy to rebuild instead of forcing output.

Independent consulting offers something employment rarely does.

Control over rhythm.

That rhythm can support a form of life balance that is difficult inside traditional structures. Not perfect balance or effortless balance, but intentional balance.

Delivery periods may be intense.

Gap periods can be restorative.

Over time, this oscillation becomes one of the quiet advantages of independence.

If every gap becomes anxiety or forced productivity, you recreate corporate pressure without corporate stability.

Used deliberately, gap periods protect not just your practice, but your energy, relationships, and long-term clarity.

Sustainability is not built on constant motion.

It is built on managed rhythm.

Economic Downturns Change Duration, Not Principles

Some gaps are short. Others stretch longer due to macroeconomic conditions.

Budgets freeze. Hiring pauses. Entire industries slow down simultaneously.

Riding Out a Downturn

Economic cycles eventually reach consulting.

In 2008, the global financial crisis slowed hiring across many industries. Projects that had been planned were postponed. New initiatives disappeared almost overnight.

For independent consultants, the pipeline can dry up quickly when companies shift into defensive mode.

During that period, I experienced the longest gap in my consulting career. Several months passed while I searched for the next project.

Fortunately, I had built some financial runway, which allowed me to stay patient and continue looking for the right opportunity. But as the months passed, the runway was getting shorter. The pressure becomes real when you are responsible for generating your own next engagement.

Eventually, an opportunity appeared. It required weekly travel and was structured as an all-inclusive rate, meaning my rate had to cover travel expenses as well as professional time.

That forced a different level of discipline.

I had to look carefully at travel costs and find ways to reduce expenses wherever possible. Instead of staying in a hotel, I rented a small apartment near the client site. It was an older building and far from luxurious, but the cost savings made the engagement workable.

The contrast was memorable.

The previous year, I had spent nearly twelve months on a project in Seattle, staying at the Westin on the fortieth floor with an incredible view of the city.

A year later, I was living in a modest apartment to control costs while rebuilding momentum.

That is part of the reality of independent consulting. Good years and lean years can exist in the same career.

The lesson was simple: be prepared to adjust quickly when economic conditions change. During downturns, flexibility and financial discipline matter as much as technical expertise.

This environment tests emotional discipline because it removes the usual feedback loop. You can do everything right and still wait.

In downturn gaps, the strategy shifts in three ways.

First, protect the runway more aggressively. Reduce discretionary burn. Do not pretend you are immune to duration.

Second, prioritize relationships with the shortest distance to demand. Former clients. Recruiters who consistently close roles. Peers who refer real work.

Third, stay professionally active without performing scarcity. Publish one useful insight. Update one asset. Have a small number of high quality conversations. Do not flood the market with signals that you are anxious.

Market contraction is not a panic signal. It is a signal to conserve structure.

Every cycle eventually shifts.

Consultants who remain composed during downturns often emerge stronger, because steadiness compounds.

The Role of the Financial Runway

Runway reduces urgency.

Urgency distorts judgment.

The consultant with runway evaluates opportunities.

The consultant without a runway reacts to them.

Gap management is not primarily about marketing.

It is about stability.

A practice that can weather a slow quarter without panic is structurally different from one that cannot.

This is why the gap reveals your true model. Not your words about the model. Your actual structure.

Runway does not need to be perfect to be useful. But it does need to be real. For many independents, three months of personal and business coverage feels tense but workable. Six months creates noticeably better decision quality. More than that creates real optionality. The exact number depends on your obligations, your market, and how quickly work tends to close in your niche.

The point is not to hit an ideal number before you ever go independent. The point is to understand what your current runway actually is, and to stop pretending uncertainty will not test it.

Runway is built during strong periods, not weak ones. That means resisting the temptation to let peak income become permanent lifestyle overhead. It means building reserves while work is abundant, because abundance is exactly when the future gap feels least real.

For consultants who do not yet have much runway, honesty matters more than pride. You may need tighter personal spending. You may need shorter planning cycles. You may need to treat the next engagement as a runway building phase rather than a reward phase.

None of that is glamorous.

All of it is stabilizing.

Runway buys something more important than comfort.

It buys judgment.

Staying Visible Without Signaling Scarcity

Visibility during gaps should feel professional, not frantic.

Simple language works.

I've recently completed an engagement and will have availability beginning next month. If you're aware of needs aligned with my background, I'd welcome the conversation.

No urgency. No defensiveness. No oversharing.

Calm signals competence.

Scarcity signaling erodes it.

If you want a quick self-check, ask this.

If I received this message from someone else, would it read as confident and selective, or would it read as anxious and open ended.

Adjust until it reads confident.

When a Gap Becomes a Pattern

Occasional gaps are normal.

Repeated, extended gaps may signal something else. Not a personal flaw. A structural issue.

Overspecialization in a shrinking niche. Weak recruiter relationships. Pricing misalignment with current demand. Sector contraction. Reputation drift.

Each one has a different response.

If you are overspecialized, broaden the way you describe outcomes without pretending you do everything. This often happens when a consultant becomes known for a narrow system area or a legacy capability that fewer organizations are investing in directly. The answer is not to abandon your expertise. It is to connect it to adjacent business problems that the market still values.

If recruiter relationships are weak, invest in a smaller set of stronger relationships rather than collecting contacts. A long list of names is not a channel. Real relationships are built through credibility, follow through, and enough repetition that people remember where you fit.

If pricing is misaligned, test your rate with new relationships while protecting your standard with established ones, and tighten scope so the rate matches responsibility. Sometimes the issue is not that your rate is too high. It is that the market reads your positioning as broader or riskier than the roles currently closing.

If the sector is contracting, shift your targeting toward industries still spending, but keep your core identity intact. A market slowdown in one segment does not require you to become someone else. It requires you to reposition intelligently.

If reputation drift is the issue, become visible through useful output, not through availability announcements. Publish something relevant. Share a practical observation. Remind the market how you think, not just that you are free.

When patterns appear, adjust deliberately. Not emotionally.

Do not abandon your model impulsively. Consciously evolve it.

Perspective

Employees rarely see volatility directly because organizations absorb it. Departments buffer it. Payroll smooths it.

Independent consultants experience volatility more visibly. At first, that can feel uncomfortable. Over time, it becomes a form of clarity.

A gap does not define your competence. It reveals your structure. It shows whether your pricing holds under silence, whether your runway protects your judgment, whether your positioning attracts aligned work, and whether your life can absorb intensity and recovery without breaking rhythm.

The goal of independent consulting is not to eliminate uncertainty. It is to become steady inside it.

Gaps are not interruptions in your practice. They are part of its design. Managed well, they sharpen thinking, protect pricing, preserve energy, and strengthen life outside the work. Misinterpreted, they create urgency where none is required.

Independent consulting becomes sustainable when you stop treating quiet weeks as danger and start treating them as structure.

The calendar will never move in a straight line. But it can move in a rhythm you understand. And once you understand that rhythm, volatility loses much of its power.

Chapter Summary

The gap is where emotional discipline and structural reality meet.

Silence invites stories. Stories create urgency. Urgency pushes consultants toward two expensive mistakes: compressing rates too quickly or accepting work they already know is misaligned.

Used well, a gap becomes design space. It is where relationships are maintained, service language is refined, assets are built, skills are sharpened, and recovery happens without apology.

Runway is what protects judgment during that period. It gives the consultant enough stability to evaluate opportunities instead of reacting to them.

The gap is not dead space between real work.

It is part of the operating model.

What Comes Next

Managing the gap well is a sign your practice has structure.

But structure is not the same as sustainability. Sustainability is the larger design question: does your model expand your options over time, or quietly consume you even when work is abundant?

The final chapter pulls the threads together and focuses on building a practice that lasts.

That is the focus of Chapter 15 - Building a Sustainable Practice.

Chapter 15
Building a Sustainable Practice

Independent consulting is not sustained by momentum. It is sustained by design.

Many consultants build successful engagements and still burn out, not because they lack demand, but because the structure of their work quietly consumes more than it returns. The calendar fills. The client is happy. The invoices get paid. And somehow, month by month, the work starts taking more than it gives.

That pattern confuses people, especially early on, because it looks like success from the outside. When you are busy, nobody worries about you. When you are busy, even you stop worrying about you. You just keep moving.

Sustainability is not accidental. It is constructed through choices that compound over time.

Sustainable practices are not louder. They are calmer.

They do not rely on hustle as a permanent operating system. They rely on a small number of repeatable behaviors that keep the work on track. You say no without guilt. You price responsibility honestly. You close cleanly. You reinvest during quieter periods. You adjust the model as life changes.

Early independence often feels like reduced choice. You take the calls. You accept the work. You convince yourself you will clean it up later.

Optionality comes later. It emerges as relationships compound, reputation stabilizes, and confidence replaces urgency.

Over time, many consultants change their model. Fewer clients and deeper engagements. Less travel and more selectivity. Narrower specialization and higher trust. Or deliberate scaling back without exiting entirely.

These shifts are not failures. They are signals of maturity.

Independent consulting works best when treated as a practice, not a hustle, not a grind, not an identity project. Practices evolve. They become quieter. They rely less on effort and more on judgment.

You are not building a job.

You are building a way of working that reflects how you think, how you decide, and how you want responsibility to show up in your life.

That is the real advantage of independence.

Sustainability is a Design Choice

Burnout in independent consulting is rarely caused by too much work. More often, it is caused by work that was never examined carefully.

Unexamined work tends to accumulate gradually. Each decision looks reasonable on its own, but the effect becomes visible only after many small choices have compounded.

You extend an engagement one more month because it feels clean and easy. You accept a small scope expansion because it helps the client and you do not want to appear difficult. You continue joining a steering meeting because it is "only" an hour. You answer the after-hours message because it is "just this once." Over time you keep holding the problem because the client has learned you will.

None of those choices feels like a turning point. Then one day something becomes obvious that should have been visible earlier.

You have been living inside other people's urgency for a long time.

The body usually recognizes it first. Fatigue appears in a way that sleep does not fix. Irritation replaces curiosity. Emotional distance becomes a substitute for structural boundaries that were never set.

This is why two consultants can earn the same income yet experience completely different levels of stress. The difference is rarely hustle. It is the design of the practice.

Design is the repeated decision to keep responsibility matched to authority, pricing, and personal energy. It is the discipline of choosing work that strengthens the practice rather than simply filling the calendar.

One practical design question can clarify a surprising amount:

Does this engagement return more than it consumes?

Not only in money, but in energy, attention, professional clarity, optionality, reputation, and rhythm.

A sustainable practice develops when consultants learn to notice work that consumes more than it returns and adjust the pattern before it becomes normal.

The Shift from Income to Optionality

Early independence is usually income-focused. The questions are practical and immediate: can I replace my salary, keep my calendar full, and survive the gaps between engagements?

Those are reasonable concerns. The problem appears when a practice remains stuck there.

Income alone does not create resilience. A consultant can earn well and still be trapped. Trapped by a single client, a single recruiting channel, or a rate that no longer matches the responsibility being carried. Sometimes the trap is less visible: a rhythm of work that leaves no space to think or recalibrate.

Resilience grows from optionality.

Optionality is simply the ability to choose.

In the early years, it is mostly imagined. Over time, it begins to appear in small, practical ways.

Optionality looks like declining work that would pay well, but would pull you into a structure you already know will drain you. It looks like taking a month away when life demands it, without your practice collapsing or your identity unraveling. It looks like ending an engagement cleanly, even when a client would prefer you to stay, because you know staying would turn you into a permanent patch.

Optionality also shows up in smaller moments: the ability to say "not yet," and mean it.

It arrives slowly. It is the compound effect of reputation, relationships, boundaries, and judgment.

A sustainable practice is one where options expand over time instead of narrowing. If your options begin narrowing, the response is not panic but curiosity. Where is dependency forming? What relationships or channels are you relying on that could disappear? What expectations are quietly expanding because they were never corrected?

Optionality is not a personality trait. It is a structural outcome of how the practice is designed.

Diversification Without Fragmentation

Many consultants hear diversification and assume it means doing more things.

In practice, healthy diversification is narrower and more intentional. It is not about collecting random work. It is about reducing single-point dependency without becoming scattered.

Fragmentation looks like chasing anything that pays. Diversification looks like building a small portfolio of aligned demand.

A fragmented practice feels like constant context switching. Different problem types, different industries with different vocabulary, different toolsets, different stakeholders, and different urgency. The work may be billable, but it rarely becomes clean. You always feel like you are starting over.

A diversified practice feels different. It may include multiple clients, but the problem shapes are similar. It may include more than one channel, but only a few, and those people understand your positioning. It may include a mix of execution and advisory work, but priced appropriately, with boundaries that protect the difference.

Think of it like architecture.

Fragmentation is adding rooms randomly because you need space. Diversification is adding structural supports so the building can handle wind.

One of the most stable designs I have seen over the years is simple. One primary lane you are known for. One adjacent lane that is credible and related. A small circle of people who know how to place you. And a set of reusable structures that keep the work clean when demand increases.

That is enough.

You do not need a broad brand. You need a focused one.

Financial Sustainability Over the Long-term

Sustainability in independent consulting is not only behavioral. It is financial.

The most durable consulting practices tend to look financially simple and, in many ways, unremarkable. This is not because the consultant lacks ambition. It is because stable finances protect judgment.

A sustainable practice assumes that gaps between engagements will occur and plans for them in advance. During strong periods, the goal is not to upgrade lifestyle quickly but to strengthen financial runway.

Independent consultants also fund infrastructure that employment previously absorbed: health insurance, retirement contributions without an employer match, training, equipment, administrative support, and the reality of nonbillable time. Recovery periods and occasional slow quarters are part of the operating model, not unexpected failures.

This is why financial simplicity often matters more than financial optimization. Highly optimized financial systems can introduce fragility. Complexity increases anxiety, and when the system becomes fragile, every gap feels personal. Rate conversations become emotional. Recruiter calls feel urgent rather than evaluative.

The goal is not to extract every possible dollar from the system. The goal is to keep the system stable enough that decisions can be made calmly.

Consultants with financial runway evaluate opportunities. Consultants without runway tend to react to them.

This is not a moral distinction. It is structural reality.

Runway reduces urgency, and urgency distorts judgment. One practical design rule follows from that principle: build the practice so that a slow quarter does not force you to accept work you already know will be misaligned.

That single capability changes the character of independent consulting.

Professional Development

Independent consultants rarely have formal development programs.

No manager assigns training. No organization outlines the next capability to build. Yet professional development remains essential.

The difference is that development becomes self-directed and closely tied to real work.

One practical approach is simple: learn from the engagement you just finished.

After each project, ask a few direct questions:

- What knowledge would have made this work easier?
- What skill gap slowed progress?
- What tool, process, or concept kept appearing in conversations?

Choose one area and deepen it before the next engagement begins.

This kind of focused development compounds over time. Instead of chasing trends or collecting certifications that never get used, consultants gradually sharpen the capabilities that their actual work demands.

Professional development also protects credibility. Clients assume independent consultants remain current in their field. Not by reacting to every industry trend, but by maintaining clear expertise in the areas where they operate.

Over time, the most effective consultants build development directly into the rhythm of their practice. Gap periods between engagements become opportunities to strengthen one capability, refine one toolset, or deepen understanding in one area that appeared during recent work.

This approach keeps development grounded in reality rather than theory.

Independent consulting rewards practical expertise more than broad familiarity. The goal is not to know everything. The goal is to remain sharp in the areas where clients depend on your judgment.

In a sustainable consulting practice, learning is not a separate activity. It becomes part of the operating rhythm of the work itself.

Quiet Confidence Replaces Urgency

As experience compounds, something subtle begins to change in how independent consultants operate.

Early in a consulting career there is often a sense of urgency. Opportunities feel scarce, so calls are answered quickly, work is accepted quickly, and boundaries are sometimes softened in the hope that momentum will continue.

Over time, pattern recognition replaces that urgency. Consultants begin to recognize misalignment earlier, trust their judgment sooner, and decline work that does not fit the structure of their practice.

This is not complacency. It is calibration.

In the early years, saying no can feel risky because it feels like another opportunity may not appear. In a mature practice, saying no becomes a normal part of maintaining alignment.

Experience makes the cost of misalignment visible. You begin to recognize the early signals: responsibility without authority, scope drifting beyond what was priced, or expectations expanding without discussion.

As this awareness grows, behavior becomes steadier. Conversations with recruiters become calmer. Scope and decision ownership are clarified before pricing is discussed. Engagements are closed cleanly rather than extended out of habit.

Gaps between engagements are no longer interpreted as failure. They are simply part of the rhythm of independent work.

Quiet confidence grows from that experience. It is not a personality trait or a temporary mood. It is the outcome of a consulting practice that has been designed carefully enough to hold under pressure.

Professional Neutrality

Independent consultants operate inside organizations without fully belonging to them. That position creates opportunity. It also creates risk.

Consultants often hear more than employees do. Frustrations are shared in private conversations. Departments quietly blame each other for stalled initiatives. Leadership decisions are debated in side meetings or hallway conversations. People may test whether you will take sides.

The temptation is subtle. Being included in those conversations can feel like acceptance. It can make you feel like part of the inner circle.

But independence depends on something different.

Professional neutrality.

A consultant's role is to solve problems, provide clarity, and support outcomes. Not to participate in internal politics, amplify grievances, or become part of the gossip economy that exists in every organization.

Once a consultant becomes associated with one faction, their usefulness to the rest of the organization declines quickly.

Integrity in consulting is not only about honesty. It is also about restraint.

Restraint in what you repeat.
Restraint in the opinions you offer about internal personalities.
Restraint in conversations that quietly pull you into alliances.

Experienced consultants learn to listen without becoming a channel for frustration. They keep client information confidential across engagements. They speak about previous clients with respect, even when projects were difficult. And they avoid casual criticism that can quietly damage a reputation.

Trust compounds slowly.

It can disappear in a single careless conversation.

The consultants who build long careers are rarely the loudest voices in the room. They are the ones people trust to handle sensitive information, maintain perspective, and stay focused on the work rather than the politics around it.

Professional neutrality protects that trust.

And trust is one of the most valuable assets an independent consultant possesses.

Knowing When to Change the Model

No consulting model lasts forever. Life changes, markets shift, energy fluctuates, and professional interests evolve.

A sustainable consulting practice allows for those shifts. Over time, many consultants discover that maintaining the practice includes occasionally redesigning how it operates.

This is where people often become stuck. The consulting model they built becomes part of their identity. Instead of adjusting it as circumstances change, they defend it and continue operating the same way, even when the environment no longer supports it.

Experienced consultants tend to take a different approach. They treat the practice as something that requires periodic maintenance and adjustment rather than something that must remain fixed.

Changing the model is not a failure. It is part of maintaining a long, sustainable practice.

Here is what changing the model can look like in real terms.

Reducing hours without exiting

For many consultants, the first meaningful evolution in independence is not leaving consulting. It is reducing hours while remaining active.

This shift is rarely achieved by simply deciding to work less. It usually happens through stronger boundaries and a tighter scope. Availability expectations become more explicit, and roles with unclear ownership are avoided.

Experienced consultants also become more deliberate about how their time is structured. Recovery time, professional positioning, and relationship maintenance are scheduled intentionally rather than squeezed between delivery work.

Waiting for space to appear rarely works. Sustainable practices create that space through clear scope, defined availability, and conscious limits on responsibility.

Shifting from execution heavy to advisory-heavy work

Moving from execution-heavy work to advisory work is rarely a single decision. It is usually a gradual repositioning.

The change often begins with language. Instead of describing the tasks you perform, you begin describing the outcomes you help clients achieve. Conversations shift from what you can do to how you help organizations make better decisions.

Your discovery process deepens as well. Advisory work requires clarity about decision ownership, authority, and the assumptions shaping the client's plans. The conversation becomes less about implementation and more about how choices will be made.

There may also be a transitional period. The market does not update its perception instantly, and some consultants experience a temporary gap while their positioning evolves.

Relationships change during this shift. Advisory opportunities tend to emerge through trust networks and prior client relationships more than through transactional recruiting channels.

Over time, the emphasis moves away from selling output toward selling clarity.

Moving from constant delivery to periodic engagements

Some consultants eventually reach a phase where continuous delivery work is no longer the goal. Instead of maintaining a full calendar year-round, they begin designing their work in seasons.

That shift requires a different structure. The practice may move toward retainers, periodic assessments, short intensive interventions, or a small number of deep engagements each year rather than constant utilization.

This transition is not about doing less. It is about designing rhythm in a way that aligns with how the consultant wants to work and live.

Returning to Employment from a Position of Strength

For some consultants, another option eventually becomes attractive: returning to employment.

This is a legitimate choice and it deserves to be named without embarrassment. Returning from a position of strength means choosing employment because it fits your life at that moment, not because independence failed.

Consultants who have worked independently often return with stronger judgment and clearer boundaries. They have experienced full accountability for outcomes, navigated uncertainty directly, and developed pattern recognition under real constraints.

Employment is not a defeat. It is simply a different operating model.

Some professionals move between independence and employment several times over the course of a career. That is not instability. It is adaptation.

Pausing without losing identity

Many independents fear pausing because they've tied their identity to staying in motion. When work slows or a gap appears, it can feel like something is wrong.

A sustainable practice does not require constant activity to remain real. Periods of adjustment, rest, or repositioning are part of the cycle of independent work.

The ability to pause without panic is a useful signal. If a pause feels manageable, the structure of the practice is likely sound. If a pause creates immediate pressure or anxiety, it usually means the practice is carrying more fragility than expected.

That realization is not something to hide from. It is information.

The most resilient consultants treat their practice as something that can be adjusted rather than defended.

Visible Risk Over Hidden Risk

One of the quiet themes running through this book is risk.

Employment often hides risk until it acts on you. Independence makes risk visible earlier. Visible risk can be evaluated. Hidden risk cannot.

Early in independence, visible risk feels like danger. You notice the signals sooner than you used to: dependence forming around your role, scope beginning to drift, responsibility expanding beyond what was priced, or the market cycle starting to shift.

That visibility is not always comfortable, but it is useful. It allows you to respond while the situation is still manageable rather than discovering the problem after it has already taken effect.

Over time, experienced consultants come to prefer visible risk. Not because it is smaller, but because it can be addressed early.

That preference reflects maturity, not bravado.

You Are Not Building a Job

One of the most common misunderstandings about independent consulting is the assumption that it simply replaces one job with another that you control.

In reality, you are not building a job. You are building a practice.

A practice is something that must be tended over time. It develops rhythms and seasons. It carries constraints that need to be respected. Its reputation is shaped by behavior rather than claims, and the relationships surrounding it strengthen when pressure is handled well. Over time, a practice also develops structures that make the work repeatable, predictable, and clean.

A job usually asks a short-term question: what do I need to do today?

A practice asks a longer question: what kind of work and reputation am I building over time?

For that reason, the goal of independent consulting is not simply to remain busy. The goal is to build a way of working that you can live inside without letting it slowly take over the rest of your life. Practices evolve as they mature. They often become quieter, more selective, and more deliberate about the work they accept and the structures they maintain.

A Closing Note

In the Preface, I described a friend who looked at the path of independence and said, "I'm not wired like you."

After years of doing this work, I have a different view of what it actually means to be wired for independence.

Looking back, independence was not a carefully engineered plan. It began with disruption. Being laid off forced me to look at my career from a different angle. What started as a practical response gradually became something more meaningful. Instead of simply finding another position, I had the opportunity to experiment with a different structure for working.

Over time that experiment became a practice. And that practice created something I had not expected at the beginning: optionality. The ability to choose which work to accept, how to structure my calendar, and how to balance professional responsibility with the rest of life.

None of that arrived immediately. Independence came with a learning curve. I mispriced work. I accepted responsibilities I should have questioned. I learned some boundaries the hard way. That process is not a flaw in the path. It is part of how judgment develops.

Looking back now, choosing independence was the best career decision I ever made.

What being wired for independence actually means is something quieter.

It is not fearlessness, and it is not a love of risk. More often, it is the willingness to notice reality early and respond calmly before small problems become large ones.

It is the discipline to keep responsibility aligned with authority and pricing. It is the ability to accept quiet periods without assuming something is wrong, recognizing that slow periods and gaps are part of the operating model and often create the space where reflection, positioning, and better opportunities emerge. It is the willingness to design rhythm in your work rather than chasing demand wherever it appears. It is also the patience to cultivate professional relationships over time, nurturing your professional circle, staying connected with peers, former colleagues, recruiters, and new contacts so that opportunities grow from trust rather than urgency.

If you are at the beginning of independence, perfection is not required. Mistakes are inevitable. You will misprice something. You will accept an engagement that should have been declined. You will discover a boundary only after it has already been crossed.

None of that is disqualifying. It is how pattern recognition develops.

The purpose of this book is not to eliminate every mistake. It is to help you recognize what is happening while you are inside it, so that you can adjust earlier, recover faster, and continue building a practice that holds.

Independent consulting becomes sustainable when you stop treating each challenge as a surprise and start recognizing it as part of the operating model.

That is the practice.

The rest comes with experience.

Chapter Summary

Independent consulting is sustained by design, not momentum.

Many consultants burn out not from lack of demand, but because the structure of their work consumes more than it returns. Sustainability is built through repeatable behaviors that keep responsibility matched to authority, pricing, energy, and rhythm.

Over time, the goal shifts from income replacement to optionality. A sustainable practice expands choice: what work you accept, when you step back, how intense periods become, and how dependent you are on any single client or channel.

Sustainability favors diversification without fragmentation, financial simplicity over fragility, steady confidence over urgency, and the ability to change the model as life changes. The deepest advantage of independence is not the absence of risk, but the ability to see it early and manage it deliberately.

Core Principles of Independent Consulting

Independent consulting is often described as freedom, flexibility, or autonomy. Those elements can exist, but they are not the foundation of the profession. The foundation is responsibility.

Over time, certain patterns become clear. Consultants who build sustainable practices tend to operate according to a small set of principles. These principles are rarely written down, but they appear consistently in the way experienced professionals approach their work.

The following principles summarize the operating logic behind independent consulting.

1. Independence Is a Structural Shift

Independent consulting is not a promotion and it is not a lifestyle upgrade. It is a structural shift in how your professional life operates.

In employment, responsibility is distributed across teams, managers, and organizational systems. In consulting, responsibility concentrates. You are accountable for clarifying scope, managing expectations, maintaining relationships, and sustaining your own pipeline.

The work itself may feel familiar. The structure surrounding the work is completely different.

2. Trust Is the Primary Currency

Consulting opportunities rarely appear because someone found a résumé online. They appear when a situation becomes uncertain and someone remembers a professional who handled pressure well.

Trust compounds through behavior. Clear communication under stress, realistic commitments, early problem identification, and consistent follow-through create professional memory. That memory often sits dormant until a new situation activates it.

When a problem appears, the question is rarely who has the best website. The question is who can step in without making the situation worse.

3. Clarity Early Prevents Conflict Later

Many consulting problems do not originate from technical failure. They originate from ambiguity.

Scope that feels "close enough" during a quick conversation becomes scope creep later. Unspoken assumptions about availability become evening and weekend work. Vague contract language becomes disagreement about responsibility.

Experienced consultants reduce these problems by creating clarity early. Confirming scope, documenting expectations, and communicating boundaries are not defensive behaviors. They are professional disciplines that protect both the engagement and the relationship.

4. Consulting Work Moves in Cycles

Independent consulting rarely unfolds in a straight line. Work appears, engagements begin, projects close, and periods between work occur.

This rhythm is normal.

Opportunities, discovery, scope definition, delivery, expectation management, closure, and the gap between engagements form a repeating cycle. Consultants do not control when opportunities appear, but they can learn to recognize where they are in the cycle and respond appropriately.

Understanding this rhythm removes much of the anxiety that early independence can create.

5. The Gap Is Part of the Model

Independent consulting includes periods between engagements. Early in the transition, these periods can feel like instability. Over time, they become recognizable as part of the operating rhythm.

The gap is not simply downtime. It is where relationships are maintained, service language is refined, and professional structure is strengthened. It is also where emotional discipline is tested. It is where capability is refined. Not through general learning, but through focused improvement in the areas that strengthen delivery.

Consultants who misinterpret the gap as failure tend to make reactive decisions. They lower rates too quickly, accept misaligned work, or change direction without enough signal.

Consultants who understand the gap treat it differently. They maintain visibility without signaling urgency. They stay connected to the right relationships. They continue refining how they describe and deliver their work.

The gap does not define the practice. How you behave within it does.

6. Sustainable Consulting Requires Balance

Consulting work operates across three modes.

Delivery mode involves execution under pressure. Systems break, deadlines approach, and clients need someone who can move problems toward resolution.

Advisory mode involves judgment. Leaders seek perspective, tradeoffs must be evaluated, and direction becomes clearer through conversation and analysis.

Positioning mode sustains the practice. Relationships are maintained, knowledge is refreshed, and future opportunities remain visible.

Too much time in any one mode creates problems. Sustainable consulting emerges from balancing all three.

7. Relationships Outlast Engagements

Projects end, but professional memory remains.

Recruiters move roles. Clients change companies. Colleagues become leaders elsewhere. The consulting profession is smaller than it first appears, and reputations travel with surprising speed.

Consultants who maintain relationships with professionalism and integrity often discover that opportunities reappear years later through unexpected channels.

The work may change. The network remains.

8. Judgment Is the Real Product

Technical expertise is essential, including a strong understanding of how systems actually function and behave in real environments. But expertise alone rarely defines the value of an experienced consultant.

Clients seek judgment. They want someone who can recognize patterns, distinguish signal from noise, identify real constraints, and recommend actions that reduce risk rather than increase it.

Over time, this judgment becomes the most valuable part of the consultant's contribution.

Independent Consultant Operating Checklist

Independent consulting does not require a complex system to operate well. It requires a small number of disciplines applied consistently.

This checklist is not exhaustive. It is a practical baseline. If these elements are in place, your practice is structurally sound.

1. Professional Structure

- Legal entity established and active
- Business banking and payment process defined
- Basic accounting and invoicing system in place
- Professional liability insurance active
- Standard contract or agreement review process defined

2. Service Clarity

- Clear description of what you do in the client's language
- Defined scope boundaries for your typical engagements
- Understanding of where you create the most value
- Ability to explain your role without relying on technical jargon

3. Recruiter and Client Relationships

- Small group of trusted recruiters you stay in contact with
- Former clients you can reach out to without hesitation
- Professional circle for calibration and perspective
- Awareness of where your next opportunity is most likely to come from

4. Engagement Discipline

- Habit of confirming scope and expectations in writing
- Clear availability boundaries, including after-hours expectations
- Understanding of how scope changes are handled
- Willingness to address misalignment early

5. Financial Stability

- Clear understanding of personal and business runway
- Awareness of monthly obligations
- Discipline to avoid reacting to short-term gaps
- Separation between income spikes and spending decisions

6. Pipeline Awareness

- Awareness of where you are in the consulting cycle
- Periodic outreach to maintain visibility without signaling urgency
- Ability to describe your availability clearly and professionally
- Avoidance of last-minute dependency on a single opportunity

7. Personal Operating Rhythm

- Ability to recognize delivery, advisory, and positioning modes
- Time set aside for administrative responsibilities
- Space for recovery between engagements when needed
- Awareness of energy levels and decision quality

How to Use This Checklist

You do not need every item perfected before you begin. But you do need awareness of where your structure is solid and where it is not.

Use this as a periodic check, not a one-time exercise.

Review it when entering a new engagement, exiting one, or when something feels off.

Gaps are not equal. Some create inconvenience. Others create pressure that will show up in your pricing, your decisions, or your ability to stay aligned in the work.

Do not try to fix everything at once.

Address the areas that reduce pressure first.

Independent consulting does not fail because of a lack of talent.

It usually breaks down where structure is missing.

A Final Thought on Independence

Independent consulting is often described in terms of freedom.

The ability to choose your work. The flexibility to shape your schedule. The opportunity to apply your experience without the constraints of a formal structure.

Those elements are real. But they are not what defines the work.

What defines independent consulting is responsibility.

Responsibility for how work enters your life. Responsibility for how expectations are set and maintained. Responsibility for how relationships are built, preserved, and sometimes repaired. Responsibility for how you respond when the situation is unclear and no one else is stepping forward to define it.

Over time, something changes.

Early in independence, much of your attention is focused on proving yourself. You think about performance, delivery, and whether you are meeting expectations. You pay close attention to signals from clients, recruiters, and the market. You wonder whether the next opportunity will appear when you need it.

That phase is normal. With experience, the focus shifts.

You begin to recognize patterns earlier. You notice when a situation is misaligned before it fully develops. You ask better questions at the beginning of an engagement. You see scope drift forming before it becomes a problem. You become more deliberate about the work you accept and the work you decline.

The work itself does not become easier. You become steadier.

That steadiness is not confidence in the sense of certainty. It is familiarity with how the work behaves over time. You have seen projects stabilize. You have seen them fail. You have experienced strong engagements and difficult ones. You have learned that both are part of the same profession.

Independence does not remove uncertainty. It changes your relationship to it.

There will be periods where work is abundant and periods where it is quiet. There will be clients who are clear and clients who are not. There will be engagements that unfold cleanly and others that require more effort than expected.

Over time, those variations stop feeling like signals about your worth.

They begin to feel like part of the rhythm.

Relationships become more important than any single engagement. The people you work with, how you show up under pressure, and how you handle difficult moments matter more than any individual project outcome.

The work compounds. Not just in skill, but in trust.

And that trust has a long memory.

I have had clients call me years later to lead system upgrades, long after the original engagement had ended. I still work with some of the same recruiters I met more than twenty-five years ago. The pattern is simple. They know how I work. I know how they operate. Over time, that mutual understanding removes friction.

Opportunities may come from unexpected places. A former client reaches out years later. A recruiter you worked with early in your career calls again. A colleague remembers how you handled a difficult situation and recommends you when something similar appears.

These moments are not random.

They are the result of patterns that were established long before.

Independent consulting has also created opportunities to work in different environments, industries, and cultures. Over time, that exposure adds up. Dozens of clients. Multiple industries. Different ways of operating. Different constraints. Different expectations. Each engagement presents a new challenge, but the underlying patterns remain consistent.

Independent consulting becomes sustainable when you focus on what actually matters: how you build relationships, how you communicate under pressure, how clearly you define scope, and how you respond when things are uncertain.

Quick Start
If You're Taking a Consulting Call Soon

Fast reference section for compressed timelines.

Independent consulting often doesn't begin with a plan. It begins with a phone call.

A recruiter reaches out. A former colleague asks for help. A client says, "We need someone now." The timeline is compressed. Context is partial. The pressure to respond feels immediate.

This section exists for those moments.

This is not a substitute for the full operating model. It is a practical reference—a way to move through early conversations calmly, professionally, and without committing yourself to responsibility you haven't evaluated yet.

Used well, it reflects the same discipline described throughout this book, applied in real time. If this is your first independent engagement, the pressure to say yes quickly is real. These questions exist to protect your judgment in exactly that moment.

If you are not actively considering a role, come back to this when the next call appears.

If you are, start here.

Before You Say Yes: Opportunity Triage

Before you evaluate rates, titles, or timelines, clarify the problem you're being asked to step into.

A few questions matter more than most others:

- What problem are they trying to solve right now?
- Who owns decisions, priorities, and approvals?
- Is this execution support, advisory judgment, or recovery?
- What does "support" actually mean in this environment?
- What assumptions might be wrong or incomplete?
- What are the actual working expectations (on-site, remote, hybrid, and travel cadence)?

You are not interrogating the opportunity.
You are clarifying reality before you commit.

The First Recruiter Call: What Actually Matters

Recruiter-led conversations move quickly by design. Rates are often mentioned early. Context arrives later.

> Your goal in the first call is not to sell yourself.
> It is to decide whether further conversation is warranted.

Listen for:

- Clarity about role versus outcome
- How decisions are made
- Whether urgency is real or habitual
- Whether expectations sound defined or assumed

Two phrases that hold the conversation without closing it:

- "Before confirming anything, I need to understand scope boundaries and decision ownership."
- "Let me clarify expectations and environment first, then I can confirm whether this is a fit."

Calm pauses signal professionalism.
They strengthen your position.

If Rate Comes Up Too Early

If rate comes up before scope is clear, a simple response works:

> "I'm flexible depending on scope and responsibility. Can you walk me through the situation first so I can give you a meaningful number?"

This is not evasion. It is precision. A rate without context protects no one.

Week One Priorities: Stability Before Speed

Once an engagement begins, week one sets the tone.

> Your highest-leverage goals are not output.
> They are clarity and alignment.

Focus on:

- Confirming environment reality (systems, versions, integrations)
- Identifying the real constraint
- Surfacing ownership gaps
- Establishing a communication cadence
- Documenting your baseline understanding in writing

A brief email to your client contact summarizing your understanding of priorities, ownership, and scope—sent by end of day Friday—creates shared memory before assumptions harden.

> Early documentation is not bureaucracy.
> It is memory protection—yours and the clients.

Three Early Traps to Watch For

Most consulting friction begins quietly.

Role drift

You are hired for support and gradually treated as the owner.
How to address it: name responsibility changes early and explicitly.

Availability expansion

Remote becomes always-on. Urgency becomes constant.
How to address it: define availability and escalation boundaries in week one.

Silent scope inflation

Small "just this once" requests accumulate into new expectations.
How to address it: force tradeoffs instead of absorbing work silently.

The Three-Question Update: Carry This Everywhere

If your update does not answer at least one of these, it is probably noise:

1. What changed?
2. Why does it matter?
3. Is a decision required?

This framework keeps communication valuable without becoming performative.
It protects your time and the client's attention.

Pause, Reset, or Exit: Know the Difference

Not every issue requires escalation. But silence almost always makes things worse.

- Pause when information is missing.
- Reset when expectations are drifting.
- Exit when responsibility exceeds authority and alignment cannot be restored.

Leaving well is a professional skill.

Staying misaligned is not loyalty, it is risk accumulation.

This Quick Start is here to orient you before urgency distorts judgment. The main chapters provide the deeper context behind these questions—and the practices that make them effective over time.

251

Appendix A
Initial Discovery Questions Before Committing

Independent consulting opportunities often appear quickly.

A recruiter calls. A former client reaches out. A project is already in motion and needs help. The timeline feels compressed, and the expectation is often to respond just as quickly.

This is where many problems begin.

Not because the opportunity is wrong, but because the situation is not yet fully understood.

Before discussing rate, start date, or commitment, take time to understand the environment you are stepping into.

The questions below are not meant to interrogate the client or recruiter. They are meant to clarify reality so you can make a sound decision.

You do not need to ask every question in every conversation. But you should have clear answers to most of them before committing.

1. Situation and Trigger

Every engagement begins with a trigger. Something changed.

- What specifically triggered the need for external help
- What is not working right now
- What has already been attempted
- What happens if nothing changes in the next 30 days
- Is this a new initiative, an upgrade, or a recovery situation

If the trigger is unclear, the scope will be unclear.

2. Problem Definition and Scope Direction

Many engagements begin with partial or assumed problem statements.

- What problem do you believe needs to be solved
- How is success currently being defined
- What would "better" look like in practical terms
- Is the problem agreed upon across stakeholders
- What is explicitly out of scope right now

If different stakeholders define the problem differently, misalignment will appear later.

3. Decision Ownership and Governance

Unclear decision ownership is one of the most common sources of friction.

- Who owns final decisions for this engagement?
- Who sets priorities when tradeoffs are required?
- Who approves scope changes?
- How decisions are communicated and documented?
- Is there a steering group, and does it make decisions or just review status?

If decision ownership is unclear, progress will slow and responsibility will drift toward you.

4. Role Expectations

The word "support" can mean very different things.

- Is this execution support, advisory guidance, or project recovery?
- What outcomes are expected from this role?
- What responsibilities are assumed but not yet stated?
- Are you expected to lead, contribute, or stabilize?
- What would success look like in the first 30 days?

Clarity here protects you from becoming responsible for work that was never defined.

5. Environment and Context

Understanding the environment reduces surprises.

- What systems, versions, and integrations are involved?
- What phase is the project currently in?
- What has already been configured, tested, or deployed?
- What constraints exist (technical, organizational, or timeline)?
- Are there known issues that are not yet resolved

You are not just stepping into a role. You are stepping into an environment that already has momentum.

6. Timeline and Urgency

Urgency is often present, but not always accurate.

- What is driving the timeline?
- Are there fixed deadlines or flexible targets?
- What happens if the timeline slips?
- Is urgency based on real constraints or accumulated delay?
- How long is the engagement expected to last?

Understanding the source of urgency helps you assess whether expectations are realistic.

7. Availability and Work Mode

Unspoken assumptions about availability often create friction later.

- What are the expected working hours?
- Are evenings or weekends expected?
- What qualifies as a true production issue?
- Is the work remote, hybrid, or on-site?
- If travel is required, how often and for how long?

If availability is not defined early, it will be defined later under pressure.

8. Team Structure and Dynamics

You are joining an existing structure, not starting from zero.

- Who are the key stakeholders and team members?
- What roles are currently filled and what gaps exist?
- Are there known areas of tension between teams?
- Who has historical knowledge of the system or project?
- Who is responsible for day-to-day coordination?

Understanding team dynamics helps you navigate the engagement more effectively.

9. Contract and Engagement Structure

Before committing, understand how the engagement is formalized.

- Is there an approved budget for this role?
- What is the expected contract structure (hourly, fixed, or hybrid)?
- What are the payment terms?
- Are there non-compete or exclusivity clauses?
- Are there restrictions related to other clients or industries?

These elements affect how you operate, not just how you get paid.

10. Risk Signals to Notice Early

Some signals appear consistently in difficult engagements.

- The problem is described vaguely but urgency is high
- Decision ownership is unclear or fragmented
- Expectations are implied rather than stated
- Multiple stakeholders are pulling in different directions
- You are expected to "figure it out" without authority

These signals do not automatically mean you should decline the work.

They mean you should proceed with clarity, structure, and explicit boundaries.

How to Use This Appendix

You do not need to run through this as a checklist in conversation.

Use it as a mental model.

The goal is simple: Understand the situation before you commit to solving it.

Independent consulting rewards clarity early.

Most problems that appear later were visible at the beginning.

They were simply not examined closely enough.

Appendix B
Statement of
Work Review Checklist

A Statement of Work defines more than deliverables.

It defines responsibility.

Many consulting problems do not begin during delivery. They begin when scope, expectations, or assumptions are accepted without being fully examined.

A scope that feels "close enough" during a fast conversation can become misaligned within weeks.

This checklist is not a legal review.

It is a practical way to confirm that what is written matches what was discussed and what you are prepared to take responsibility for.

1. Role and Scope Alignment

Start with the most important question.

Does the written scope match your understanding of the role?

- Does the description reflect what was discussed in conversations?
- Is your role clearly defined as execution, advisory, or recovery?
- Are responsibilities stated clearly, not implied?
- Is there any language that expands your role beyond what was discussed?

If the written scope is broader than the conversation, clarify before signing.

2. Deliverables and Outcomes

Vague deliverables create open-ended responsibility.

- Are deliverables clearly defined?
- Are outcomes described in practical terms?
- Are success criteria stated or implied?
- Are timelines or milestones included where appropriate?

If deliverables are unclear, you are accepting responsibility without boundaries.

3. Exclusions and Boundaries

Most problems come from what is not written.

- Does the SOW clearly state what is out of scope?
- Are adjacent responsibilities explicitly excluded?
- Is there a process for adding new scope?
- Are you protected from absorbing unrelated work?

If exclusions are missing, assume expectations will expand.

4. Decision Ownership

Responsibility without authority creates risk.

- Who owns final decisions?
- Who sets priorities when tradeoffs arise?
- Who approves scope changes?
- Is governance structure defined or implied?

If decision ownership is unclear, you may become the default owner.

5. Availability and Work Expectations

Unspoken expectations become pressure later.

- Are working hours defined?
- Are after-hours expectations stated?

- Is on-call or incident support expected?
- Are response time expectations defined?

If availability is not defined, it will be defined during escalation.

6. Travel Expectations

Travel changes both cost and effort.

- Is travel required or optional?
- How often is travel expected?
- Are duration and location defined?
- Who covers travel expenses?
- Is travel time billable?

If travel is mentioned but not defined, clarify before committing.

7. Rate and Payment Terms

Clarity here prevents unnecessary friction.

- Is the rate clearly stated?
- Are billing terms defined (hourly, daily, milestone)?
- What are payment terms (net 15, net 30, etc.)?
- Are there approval steps before invoicing?
- Is there any holdback or conditional payment language?

If payment depends on unclear conditions, resolve it early.

8. Contract Restrictions

These clauses can affect your ability to operate.

- Are there non-compete clauses?
- Is there exclusivity language?
- Are there restrictions on working with similar clients?
- Are duration and geographic limits defined?

If you have existing or prior clients in similar spaces, clarify exclusions explicitly.

9. Intellectual Property and Ownership

Understand what happens to your work.

- Who owns deliverables created during the engagement?
- Whether the agreement includes work-for-hire language?
- Whether you can reuse your own frameworks, templates, or approaches in future engagements?
- Whether any restrictions apply to materials you bring into the engagement?

Independent consultants often carry methods, templates, and experience from one engagement to another. Make sure the agreement does not unintentionally restrict your ability to reuse them.

10. Termination and Exit Conditions

Every engagement ends. The question is how:

- Can either party terminate the agreement?
- What notice period is required?
- What happens to work in progress?
- Are there penalties or obligations at termination

A clean exit structure protects both sides.

11. Scope Change Mechanism

Scope will change. The question is whether it is controlled.

- Is there a defined process for scope changes?
- Are changes documented and approved?
- Does pricing adjust with scope?
- Is additional work explicitly authorized?

If no mechanism exists, scope will expand informally.

12. Consistency Check

Before signing, pause and ask one question: Does this document reflect the reality I expect to operate in?

If the answer is no, clarify before proceeding.

How to Use This Appendix

You do not need to review every clause in detail.

Focus on alignment.

The goal is simple:

Make sure what is written matches what was discussed and what you are willing to own.

Independent consulting does not require perfect contracts.

It requires clear understanding.

Most scope problems are visible at the beginning.

They were simply not questioned early enough.

Appendix C
Scope Clarification Email Example

Most consulting misalignment does not begin with bad intent.

It begins with different interpretations.

A short, well-written email at the beginning of an engagement can prevent weeks of confusion later.

This is not a formal document.

It is a simple confirmation of your understanding.

Its purpose is to create shared clarity before assumptions harden.

When to Send This

Send this after:

- Initial discovery conversations
- Verbal agreement on role and direction
- Before or immediately after starting the engagement

Do not wait until problems appear.

Clarity is most effective at the beginning.

What This Email Does

A good scope clarification message does two things:

It creates shared memory.

It makes scope drift visible when expectations begin to change.

Example — Clean Scope Confirmation

Subject: Confirmation of Role, Scope, and Expectations

Based on our recent conversations, here is my understanding of the role and scope for this engagement.

The focus will be on:

- Stabilizing the current manufacturing and planning processes
- Identifying root causes of recent system and operational issues
- Supporting the team in restoring a reliable operating rhythm

This role is focused on execution and stabilization within the current environment.

This engagement does not include:

- Broader system redesign
- New module implementation
- Ownership of project management unless we agree to expand scope

Decision ownership will remain with your internal leadership team. I will provide recommendations and support execution within the agreed scope.

Standard availability will be during business hours in the agreed time zone. After-hours support will be limited to true production-related incidents.

The engagement is expected to be primarily remote, with approximately three to four site visits as discussed.

If any of these points do not align with your expectations, please let me know so we can adjust before moving forward.

Appendix D
Weekly Status and Expectation Reset

Most consulting issues do not come from a lack of effort.

They come from drift.

Priorities shift. Assumptions change. New stakeholders appear. Small requests accumulate. What was once clear becomes implied.

A short, structured weekly update prevents that drift from becoming misalignment.

This is not about reporting activity.

It is about maintaining alignment.

What This Update Does

A strong weekly update does three things:

- Reinforces what actually moved
- Surfaces what is unclear or blocked
- Forces decisions before issues expand

It keeps expectations visible.

When to Send It

End of each week (recommended)

- After a major milestone or shift
- When priorities or expectations begin to drift

Consistency matters more than format.

The Simple Structure

If your update does not answer at least one of these, it is likely noise:

1. What changed
2. Why it matters
3. What decision is needed

Everything else is optional.

Example: Weekly Alignment Update

Subject: Weekly Update — Status and Alignment

Here is a summary of progress and current focus areas for this week.

What moved:

- Identified the root cause of planning inconsistencies in the current setup
- Aligned with the operations team on immediate stabilization steps
- Began validating configuration changes in the test environment

What matters now

- Stabilization efforts are progressing, but the current configuration limits flexibility in planning
- Additional changes may be required depending on test results next week

What is blocked or unclear:

- Confirmation needed on priority between short-term stabilization and longer-term process adjustments
- Access to historical data is still pending

Issues and concerns (if applicable):

- Current configuration may limit scalability if not addressed early
- Unclear decision ownership could slow progress as scope expands

Decisions needed:

- Confirm whether to prioritize immediate fixes or begin parallel work on structural improvements
- Confirm timeline expectations for next phase

Current focus for next week:

- Complete testing of configuration changes
- Implement approved adjustments
- Continue coordination with operations and planning teams

If any of the above does not align with your expectations, please let me know so we can adjust direction early.

Why This Works

This structure is effective because it is:

- Focused
- Decision-oriented
- Easy to read
- Difficult to ignore

It avoids long status reports that create the appearance of progress without clarity.

Variations by Engagement Type

Execution-heavy roles

Emphasize:

- Progress against tasks
- Issues and blockers
- Immediate next steps

Advisory roles

Emphasize:

- Insights and tradeoffs
- Implications of decisions
- Recommended direction

Recovery situations

Emphasize:

- What is being stabilized?
- What remains at risk?
- What requires immediate attention?

Common Mistakes to Avoid

Listing activity instead of progress
Work completed does not always equal movement.

Avoiding uncomfortable topics
If something is unclear or misaligned, this is where you surface it.

Overloading detail
Long updates reduce clarity and lower response rates.

Skipping weeks
Inconsistency allows drift to build unnoticed.

How This Prevents Problems

This update creates a consistent reference point.

When expectations begin to shift, you can point back to prior alignment and reset direction without conflict.

It also changes how you are perceived.

You are not just doing the work.

You are managing clarity.

How to Use This Appendix

You do not need a complex reporting system.

You need a repeatable habit.

A short, structured weekly update keeps the engagement aligned, reduces unnecessary friction, and prevents small issues from becoming larger problems.

This is one of the simplest disciplines in independent consulting.

It is also one of the most effective.

Appendix E
Closing an Engagement Professionally

Every consulting engagement ends.

The work may conclude as planned. The client may shift direction. The budget may change. Or the engagement may simply reach its natural stopping point.

How you leave matters.

The end of an engagement is not just a transition. It is a signal. It shapes how the client remembers the work, whether your name is recommended, and whether the relationship continues.

A professional close is not complex. It is deliberate.

1. Confirm the End Clearly

Do not let an engagement fade out informally.

- Confirm the final date of active work
- Clarify what remains in scope through that date
- Identify any work that will not be completed

Ambiguity at the end creates unnecessary confusion. Clarity creates confidence.

2. Align on What Was Completed

Before closing, make sure there is shared understanding of what was delivered.

- What was completed?
- What was stabilized or improved?
- What remains open or in progress?
- What decisions were made?

This is not about claiming credit. It is about leaving a clear record.

3. Document Open Items and Risks

No engagement ends with everything resolved.

What matters is visibility.

- List any unresolved issues
- Identify risks that may affect future work
- Note dependencies that remain in place
- Clarify what requires follow-up

Unspoken issues do not disappear. They become future problems.

4. Transfer Knowledge Cleanly

Make it easy for the client to continue without you.

- Provide documentation where needed
- Ensure key contacts understand the current state
- Walk through important processes or decisions
- Confirm access to relevant systems or materials

A clean handoff reflects professionalism. It also reduces follow-up questions later.

5. Close Communication Professionally

Your final communication sets the tone for how the engagement is remembered.

A simple closing message can include:

- Appreciation for the opportunity

- Summary of contributions
- Acknowledgment of the team
- Clarity on availability after the engagement

Keep it straightforward. This is not a sales message.

6. Preserve the Relationship

The relationship does not end when the work ends.

- Stay connected without forcing contact
- Respond professionally if questions arise later
- Leave the door open for future work

Many consulting opportunities return through prior clients. How you leave determines whether that happens.

7. Leave the Environment Better Than You Found It

This is the simplest measure of a successful engagement.

Not perfection.

Improvement.

Systems clearer. Decisions cleaner. Direction more defined.

That is what clients remember.

A Simple Closing Check

Before you consider the engagement complete, ask:

- Is there clarity on what was done and what remains?
- Can the client move forward without confusion?
- Have risks been made visible?
- Would they call me again?

If the answer is yes, the engagement is complete.

Final Thought

The end of an engagement is usually the end of the work.

What matters is whether you leave the relationship with clarity, professionalism, and trust intact.

If you do, you have planted a seed that may produce future opportunities.

ood-product-compliance

716

874409*